The Shipyard Apprentice

BEST REGARDS
WILLIE

Willie Scott

01/03/2012

W & R Scott

Published by
W & R Scott
Nairn, IV12 5BD
www.wrscottpublishing.co.uk

cover photograph courtesy Harland and Wolff

ISBN 978-0-9570994-0-1

Printed and bound in England by
www.printondemand-worldwide.com

Dedication and acknowledgements

I have dedicated this book to my wife Ruth who has looked after me for many years since having rheumatoid arthritis, and to Dr Steven, Dr Harvey, and Mr Finlayson of Raigmore Hospital Inverness, who saved my life a wee while ago.

Also to Sister Lyn Forbes, Doctor Slater, nurses, physios and OT at The Highland Rheumatology Unit in Dingwall; who persevered with a grumpy old man and got me to walk again after being bedridden for five months. This enabled me to walk my daughter Nicole down the aisle, my other daughter Caroline being bridesmaid, one step behind lest I tripped.

My thanks to all these people and also to David McVeigh, Sales Manager at Harland and Wolff for supplying the cover photo of *Methane Progress* on slips in 1964; a ship I worked on whilst serving my time at Harland and Wolff, Queen's Island Belfast in the 1960s.

Contents

Chapter 1

MY FIRST DAY

It was a bright autumn morning as I stepped out on my first day to work. I was walking along the old familiar railway path to catch the 6.30am train to Belfast, at last starting my long awaited career as an apprentice in the shipyards of Harland & Wolff.

I grew up in Bangor; a quiet small town on the shores of Belfast Lough and on this special day was as happy as the day was long; but about to have my eyes opened to the outside world.

The year was 1962 and I was almost sixteen. I had just finished college and was raring to get on with life, especially as serving my time in the yard would lead eventually to my ambition to go to sea. My father, grandfather and most of their family had been fishermen, so the salt water was rattling through my veins at a great rate of knots. I loved the sea, boats, fishing and was daft on anything remotely mechanical; motor bikes, engines, cars, and steam trains. These all held a great appeal to me.

However, today I was kitted out in jeans, hobnailed boots, donkey jacket (which was the height of fashion in the early '60s), flat cap, overalls under one arm and lunchbox under the other. The lunchbox held a treat as today's piece was a couple of sandwiches of meat left over from Sunday roast. These sandwiches were wrapped up in grease-proof loaf wrapping paper and put into my new cream tin lunchbox, its green tin lid held down with a rubber band made from an old bike inner tube.

My mother had bought me two pairs of brown overalls, and as usual like most of my jeans they were too long for me and had been turned up at the legs. Ma's famous old saying, 'you will grow into them and they will fit better when they have been washed a few times' gave me many a red face in my teenage years. The

7

overalls were in fact well patched and washed before they shrunk, and then when the legs were finally let down showing the unworn cloth 'extensions' to the old worn legs, led to much amusement and a few wise cracks at the time by my work-mates at the yard.

I was the youngest of a family of six; having two sisters and three brothers. Ma worked a few hours a day cleaning for a posh lady, in the Ward Park area, a very select part of the town. Dad had given up the fishing boat a while ago and was now a "ganger" on a building site as well as part- time coastguard. My eldest sister Margaret, who I had called Mags for as long as I could remember, worked in a local sweet factory, making Foxes Glacier Mints – we never wanted for mints! My eldest brother Frankie was a piano tuner in Gilpins of Belfast and he rode a much guarded 197cc Francis Barnett two stroke motorbike. My other sister Beth worked as a shop assistant in a cake shop in Bangor; the next youngest brother Johnny worked at the Short's aircraft factory in Sydenham as a draftsman (Short's was to become part of Belfast City Airport). Johnny often helped me with my homework, always with great patience and many a late night I sat with him as he explained the com-plications of mechanical drawing, getting through about half a loaf of bread in the process. (Bread was great for rubbing out pencil mistakes; you can never find a rubber when you need one.)

My other brother Robert, who was about five years older than me, and to whom I was very close, was at sea in the merchant navy. Hence the lure of the sea, passed down through the generations of Scott's bade me follow him to sea as ships' engineer.

I walked into the station ticket office and asked for a weekly return to Belfast. This ticket would last me all week and cost twelve shillings and sixpence, a right chunk out of my promised starting wages of three pounds and sixpence, but still a fortune compared to my old paper round wage of ten bob! The train came into view round the last bend in the railway track and blew its two-tone air horn, a far cry from the days of steam trains when the engine driver blew the steam whistle to hurry the latecomers along the railway path and, to warn the waiting passengers to keep clear of the edge of the platform.

As a child I used to be scared stiff of the steam train as it screeched to a halt amid clouds of hissing steam. My Uncle Jim was Station Master at Helen's Bay and had a house right beside the track. Aunt Clara was a great cook and she used a wood stove with an oven to cook on. Cousin Alison and I were close friends from early childhood and remain so fifty odd years later.

Anyway, as I got older I became very attracted to the steam trains; the squeal of

8

the brakes, black power cylinders hissing steam and water. But most of all the never to be forgotten smells from a mixture of coal smoke, steam, hot cinders, oil and sleeper tar as the train slowed and squealed to a stop alongside the platform.

There were quite a few passengers waiting as the train drew up to the platform and, as the automatic doors opened with a hiss of compressed air, we climbed aboard into the carriages and sat down. I always liked facing towards the front as a child as my Da used to say 'Likes to see where he is going – not where he has been'. The train was quite crowded as my station was the second from Bangor town station and a lot of the passengers who were from the town were already on board, reading their morning papers.

We stopped at every station on the way to Belfast, workers coming on in ones and twos; most of them worked at the shipyard or the aircraft factory, but some also worked at the spinning mills on the outskirts of the Belfast. A lot of the passengers got off at Sydenham Station, which was close to the aircraft factory, and even more at the next stop; Ballymacarratt Halt that was just across from "The Oval" Irish League Glentoran's football ground and close to the Sydenham Road shipyard entrance gates at Dee Street.

I remained on the train as the directions I had got at my interview were from the Belfast Station and, once there, stepped into the station and out onto the coal quay where Kelly's coal-boats unloaded the coal shipped from Scotland and Wales. (My Da used to say that the coal-boats would sail even if the haystacks were being blown across the fields) The road ran past the quay and on through the Main Shipyard Security Post and I walked through the gates into the shipyard.

I had about a fifteen-minute walk and the footpaths were full of men all going the same way. The roads were also busy, most of the traffic being busses, motorbikes, pushbikes, and a few cars; invariably black Austin's and Morris's. A lot of the men wore flat caps, known as dunchers, and carried their lunchbox under their arm; some carried a paper, probably the Belfast News Letter. They walked with an assured swagger of the shoulders and talked out of the side of their mouths, from which hung a half-smoked woodbine.

At last I came to Harland & Wolff Training School, a large building like a warehouse with offices on one end. The door was open and I went straight in and reported to a man in a suit and black bowler hat. I was later to discover that the bowler hat signified a 'gaffer' and they were to be avoided if at all possible as they always gave out work, even if you were already busy.

'What can I do for you boy?' the Bowler with a very jagged Belfast accent asked me.

'I am to report for work as an apprentice,' I replied in a rather shaky, high pitched voice.

'Not from the town then? Name and trade!' he bawled

At least it sounded like he bawled, but I later found out that this was the way of talking in the shipyard, as it was so noisy on the slips and in the workshops, everybody shouted. In later years my hearing started to diminish and I was told that this was due to the constant pounding of my eardrums by the noise in the shipyard and engine rooms of ships. In those days there were no earplugs or muffs; at least I never saw any.

'William Scott from Bangor. I am to learn to be a marine fitter, and I want to go to sea!' I replied, still pretty intimidated by the Bowler.

'Well Scott, stay with us and you will get the best training in the world and be taught all you ever need to know about ships and engines. Go through there and put your overalls on, then join the queue over at that office. Come down to the bottom of the workshop when you are through.'

I got into my overalls and joined a queue of about fifty other lads, waiting to go into an office.

'Your first day as well?' asked a small dark-haired lad beside me, whom I thought I recognised.

'Yes, first day, what are you going to be?'

'Electrician, didn't you play football for Bangor Tech?' says he.

'Yes,' I replied. 'I still play for the BB.'

'I thought I recognised you from somewhere.'

'I am up to be a marine fitter,' I said proudly. It turned out that we had played football against each other in teams in the County School League, and the Boys Brigade League.

'Next!' bawled a wee baldy headed man from inside the office.

'My name's Scott.'

'Right,' says Baldy, 'read this and sign at the bottom, Mr Raynor will witness your signature.'

I hadn't noticed anyone else in the office but over in another corner a very uncompromising looking man sat behind a large leather-covered desk. He was dressed in a dark pinstriped suit, like the elders in the church wore, and had specs perched on the end of a large red nose. I read through the paper, which was written in copperplate and turned out to be my Indentures. I gave due consideration to the paragraph about misconduct, bad timekeeping and obedience to those in authority, which Baldy had put his finger on, and signed at the bottom. I then took the papers over to Pin Stripe with the nose, for countersigning.

'Have you noted the paragraph regarding misconduct, your apprenticeship will be terminated on any; and I mean any of these misdemeanours?' I nodded, too dumbstruck to speak to God! 'This will be one of the most important documents you will ever sign, I wish you luck,' he said with a cough which knocked an ash about two inches long of the fag in his gub. He then dismissed me with an absent-minded wave of his hand, as if he was swatting flies.

I wondered how many lads like I had stood trembling in front of him as he countersigned the indentures, with a flourish of his gold-nibbed Parker. He must be a real big shot at the yard and I bet he has a special bowler hat I thought. He turned out to be the Apprentice Manager for the whole shipyard and held in awe by all the apprentices, and not a few of the old hands.

I saw him several times whilst in the training centre and also when I was in the engine works. He had a white dustcoat over his suit, but just an ordinary black bowler on his head. He nodded at the men and apprentices as he passed by but never recognised me, of course.

I passed on out of his office into the workshop. This was laid out much the same as the technical college workshop, only on a much larger scale. Steel screens about five feet high divided the workshop into two halves lengthwise. All along one side were heavy wooden benches, with an engineers' vice at each corner and a drawer under the vice, which was, I presumed for our tools.

The other side of the workshop was taken up fully by machines. I could see quite a few lathes, a shaping machine, a couple of mechanical saws, and a few machines that I hadn't seen, let alone used before. I couldn't see what was in the area behind the screens, but found out later that this was the shipwrights and electricians area.

There were three other new fitters and we were allocated a bench to ourselves. As we took our places, there were stares from the other lads who had been there for a few months, but they didn't look an unfriendly bunch, as I had feared.

Across from us were the boys training to be machinists and turners, they worked away without lifting their heads from their machines, as I had been taught to do at the technical college. Full concentration was needed if mistakes were not to be made or, worse still, get caught up in the moving parts. We three new fitters intro-duced ourselves and then stood rather self-consciously waiting to be told what to do. Presently an instructor, wearing a brown dustcoat over flannels and shirt and tie, again with a black bowler hat on his head, came across to us.

'I am Michael Fullerton; you will call me Mr Fullerton. I am in charge of youse apprentice fitters and you will be here for a full 12 months.'

He went on to tell us that during this time we would be trained mainly in the use of bench tools, but would also spend some time on lathes and other machinery.

I knew I had five years to serve, so I was here in the training centre for a year and then outside to the slips, fabrication shops and engine-works, the latter of which I had indicated on my application form and interview, as my preference. The engine works was the department where the diesel engines were produced, assembled and tested.

Mr Fullerton gave us each a tool kit, consisting of files, engineers square, steel rule, dividers and some other small hand tools, and a lock for our drawers.

'Lose any tools, locks or keys and it will come off your wages,' he warned.

He then took us through to the classroom and showed us a film on safety in the workplace, which I found pretty boring and nearly fell asleep. Well, I had been up since 5am that morning!

At last it was dinnertime and we went round to one of the works canteens. I lined up with my football chum, whose name was Harry, and we chatted away about the morning's activities. Harry, the apprentice electrician had been given a lot more tools than I had; all 'insulated' he told me knowingly. He had seen the same film, along with his intake of new electricians, and enjoyed it; no accounting for taste

I got a mug of soup and sat down with Harry at a table almost full of older apprentices, some from the training school but mostly from the outside works. I took my hat off to eat, but most of the others kept theirs on.

'Where are you from, with your fancy manners?' sprayed one of the older boys, with his mouth full.

Before I could reply another said, 'Looks like a Taig to me,' and stared stone-faced right at me.

I was struck dumb.

'He is from Bangor and he is not a Catholic, he is in the BB,' said Harry, coming to my rescue.

I was very thankful for this intervention by Harry, and even more so that he remembered I was in the Boys Brigade. I asked Stone Face what difference was it if I was a Catholic; he answered in no uncertain terms,

'This table is for Prods only, in fact there are very few Taigs even allowed to work in the yard.'

'Don't bother me at all' I replied, starting to get annoyed.

'Me neither' said Harry, backing me up.

Stoneface just shrugged and looked knowingly at his mates.

I asked Stoneface for the salt and he passed it over to me. I shook it over my mug of soup and to my horror the top came off and the whole contents poured into my soup!

'Take soup with your salt, fancy boy?' asked Stoneface with a big smirk like a catfish on his face.

I saw red, and before Harry could stop me I lunged across the dinner table at him narrowly missing his right lug and tipping his tea into his lap in the process.

'No need to lose the ould head Bangor! You have severely curtailed my sex life,' he said looking down at his soaked trousers whilst trying to laugh it off.

'That's a tanner you owe me for the soup,' I said rising slowly from the table and heading back into the dinner line.

'Nice one son, he's needed that for a while. His Da is a Grand Master of a Shankill Lodge, and thinks he is the bee's knees. Tell that ould doll on the till that this is a replacement mug of soup and you don't have to pay for it,' said the dinner lady.

'Thanks missus, I am starving and lost the head a wee bit when my soup got ruined,' I replied heading on down the line.

When I got back to the table, yer man was away but, he had left a tanner beside my lunchbox.

Thus I was initiated into the brotherhood of the shipyard workers. I also had been enlightened on their views on Catholic workmates, although, I was to hear different views from other workers whilst serving my time.

Where I was brought up we didn't mix much with Catholics, in fact it was even regarded as bad luck to be passed by a priest, usually on an old bike with his black robes flapping about his ankles. There was never any malice in it; Catholics went to the Catholic school we Protestants went to the Protestant schools and our paths seldom crossed.

We commemorated King William's crossing the Boyne in 1690 every 12th of July by burning a bonfire and watching the orange parade, but apart from that we lived and let live.

I never got to know any Catholics well until I went to the technical college where for the first time there were boys of mixed religion. I remember that at the start of every school day the Catholics would leave the room for their own religious instructions. We would have about ten minutes religious instruction then start the morning lessons; half an hour would pass before the Catholics would return to class.

Back at work after lunch the instructor took us through the next four weeks' work, starting by giving us a block of metal to file square. This nearly took up the first week because as soon as one side was square I would take too much of the other side and have to start all over again! At five minutes to five we all trooped up to the toilets to wash our hands and change out of our overalls. We then lined up at the time clock to clock off. At five' o'clock exactly, a hooter, not unlike a ships foghorn, sounded loudly very close by, causing most of us new boys to jump nearly out of our skins. As I punched my card in the time clock I realised that I had completed my first day and, was still in one piece; despite all the rumours I had heard about the hard men in the shipyard. I had also been given a nickname – Bangor!

Emerging from the training school doors I found myself in the middle of a stampede of men, bikes, busses and cars all going in different directions at breakneck speed and with a roar not unlike the sound of the start of the Ulster Grand Prix. In the midst of all this mayhem stood a solitary traffic policeman, complete with holstered gun, wearing the biggest pair of white gloves I had ever seen.

I pushed my way into the throng, got shoved in the wrong direction and nearly got run over twice when I slipped on tram lines embedded in the cobbles of the road. I had never seen tram lines before and have been wary of them ever since, especially when on a motorbike. I eventually made it to the train station; only to find that I had missed my train by about five minutes, so had to wait another twenty minutes for the next one. Still it had been an eventful day I reflected, as I sat down on the station bench mulling over the events of the day. I found I had quite enjoyed the yard and was looking forward to whatever tomorrow would bring.

I arrived home just on six' o'clock and as I walked up the back garden path; the smell of beef stew wafting from our kitchen greeted me.

'How did you get on son? I was thinking about you all day,' asked Ma. 'Mrs Brown (the posh lady Ma worked for) said that they all talk different in Belfast. Go and wash your hands well and sit down at the table, dinner is just about ready.'

'I got on well at work but missed the early train. Still, the train I caught wasn't so crowded and didn't stop at every hole in the hedge. We stopped at every station between here and Belfast this morning.'

'That's because the one you came home on was an express so you are only about ten minutes later than we thought you would be,' Da said, looking over the top of the *Belfast Telegraph*, known locally as the Telly.

One by one the rest of the family arrived home from work and sat at the table. Ma ladled out the stew and I put big dollops of HP sauce on mine, blowing on it to cool it down enough to eat. We had milk, or buttermilk to drink with our dinner; I always had buttermilk, as I liked it ever since I had worked on my uncle's farm near Groomsport, about four miles from Bangor. Although this 'Co-op' milkman's buttermilk was a bit thinner than the real thing, it still tasted great.

Frankie, my eldest brother, said that there were people throwing stones at the 'B' specials and police in Belfast.

'You stay away from all that trouble,' ordered Da, pointing down the table at Frankie.

'It is hard to avoid when you are caught in the middle of it,' said Frankie, 'we were delivering a piano to a house at the bottom of the Falls Road when all hell let loose. The women were shouting and throwing stones and bottles at the police. One of the van boys got his shin cut on a flying stone and there was broken glass scattered all along the pavements, I hope the trouble won't come to Bangor!'

'No chance of that,' replied Johnny. 'We are much too sensible down here, and there are not many Catholics in Bangor anyhow.'

'What difference does that make?' I asked.

'Well you see son,' said Da 'for many years the Catholics have not been happy with the way they are being treated and want us to join with the Free State. The first chance they get they show this by fighting with the Protestants, 'B' specials and police. There is talk of the English sending over soldiers to keep them all apart and stop the fighting.'

'I don't know where it will all end,' cried Ma, 'you make sure and keep yourself to yourself in that shipyard William. There are a lot of hard bitter men working there.'

After dinner I went up to my friend Noel's house for a chat. As usual we stood outside his door or sat on his step.

'How did you get on with the townies then, Willie?' he asked.

'Oh all right I suppose, some hard men with long sideburns. They are right down on the Catholics and I nearly got into a row about it. Do you remember a boy called Harry who used to play for Hollywood in the school league? Well he baled me out; he is a right wee terrier and a good mate to have.'

'Yes, I mind him; played on the wing, didn't take any prisoners. We don't bother about religion and all that at work, there is a few Catholics working on the building site,' replied Noel (my Da had got him started in the building trade as a plasterer.) 'We just get on with the job no matter what religion we are.'

I told Noel about my row over the soup and he told me to be careful as these boys had stacks of mates, who he had heard, were very hard men.

I said cheerio to him and went back home to get washed and ready for band practice at the Boys Brigade hall. As usual after practice we ended up in Toni's café and I told my friends how I got on at my first day at work. I looked enviously at the Triumphs, Norton's and BSA's on their stands outside the café, wondering if I would ever be able to afford one. I drank up the last of my frothy coffee from the bottom of the Pyrex cup, amazed at the difference in taste from the 'Camp Coffee' we got at home.

We all cast covetous glances at the bikers in their black leather jackets, white scarves and light blue jeans tucked into shining leather bike-boots. Then there was their girlfriend's who always seemed to be chewing gum, had enormous eyelashes and wore tight jumpers and jeans. They stood beside the jukebox, listening or jiving with each other to the rock'n'roll music they played over and over again. I preferred Jim Reeves, Dusty and Elvis; later on of course it was the Beatle's and Stone's records we played.

There wasn't much happening in the café so I said goodnight to the lads and walked up home. I had a quick cup of tea whilst watching my sister Mags making up everyone's sandwiches for the morning.

'Did you enjoy your piece today?' asked Mags.

'Yes it was great,' I replied, 'I kept the loaf paper in my lunchbox so you can use that again. What's for tomorrow?'

'Spam and tomato sauce, I've made you plenty and there is a wee bit of fruit bun that Beth brought home from the cake shop.'

'Dead on, I am off to bed now as I am really tired, see you tomorrow night, goodnight Ma and Da,' I said as I climbed the stairs.

'Night, night, son – you will remember this day for a while,' said Da.

How right he was!

Chapter 2

BACK TO SCHOOL

Once I had clocked in the next morning I was told to go to the classroom for a talk on the safe use of tools. After the talk, which was interesting but mostly stuff we took for granted, the instructor told us about day release and night school.

I hadn't forgotten about this clause of the indentures, (Attendance of day release and night school is Mandatory!) but I thought it would be a while before it started. However the instructor gave each of us attendance cards, which had to be stamped by the college on the mornings and afternoons and the two nights of night school. I was to attend the technical college from which I had so recently escaped, every Wednesday – all day! As well as Tuesday and Thursday nights from 7 pm to 9.30pm.

This was quite a blow, not only going back to school so soon, but also missing two nights at the BBs. There was no way round this and the instructor had the gall to tell us we were very fortunate to be given this chance of further education, especially as at the end of four years we would receive a City and Guilds Certificate. This certificate would prove to the company that we were smart young men, good enough for the design and drawing offices and would eventually gain promotion. Yuk! I viewed these people in shirts and ties as totally square, with no go in them at all. However, it was all part of the training and would help with my grading on entrance to the Merchant Navy, so I suppose it was best to go along with the rest of the lads.

Wednesday morning, a lie on till eight o'clock and a leisurely breakfast, this was more like it! I went out the back door and onto my old pushbike and set off for college, waving every so often to friends who had stayed on at school sitting highers in the hope of a better career.

'Well, would you look at what the cat dragged in?' announced the teacher as I entered the classroom.

'Morning sir, nice to be back.' I don't think, under my breath.

'How are you getting on at the yard?' He asked, too pleasantly.

'Not too bad so far sir, but I have only been at work for a couple of days, before being told to come back to school.'

'It's not called school now,' he bawled.

Here we go I thought; some things never change, he will start huffing and puffing and his face will go red. He was on canteen duty one day before I left school and I accidentally knocked over a bottle of milk!

'Who spilt the milk!' he shouted, leaping about like someone possessed. (His nickname was 'Jack the leaper'.) Of course all hell broke out, everyone repeating what he had shouted and saying that you shouldn't cry over spilt milk, and the like. As usual I got the blame of it. Two knuckles over the head for me; and they wonder why I was so glad to escape to the shipyard.

'You are a big boy now and are attending 'Day Release' to further your education,' he gasped, 'although going by your track record, it will be a waste of time. Sit down and get out your books.'

I looked round at the other boys in the class, there were only about ten or twelve of us and he pointed to the very front seat (which I had occupied for the previous two years and which incidentally, had been occupied by my brother Robert when he was at the Tech.)

Some release, I thought, I'd rather be at the yard any day than taking bull from this particular teacher! Somehow the morning went in and I joined a few other lads in the old air-raid shelters for the crack, it was covered in smoke from Woodbine smokers. I had given up smoking (such as it was – about one a week, and maybe a few of my Da's old butts) when I started playing football for the school.

'How's it going, Willie?' asked one of the lads.

'Dead on, I am at the shipyard now, and only here on day release,' I replied quite loudly in order to advertise the fact.

'Want a fag?' he offered.

'Thanks, might as well, everybody smokes in the yard,' I told him.

I cadged a light, and felt quite a lot older as I inhaled the smoke, blowing it out in what I thought was a very professional manner (but actually feeling a bit boakey and light-headed). I wondered if I would be allowed to smoke in the house, but decided there and then not to risk it as I would probably get a clip round the ear from Da, even though he smoked over twenty 'Gallagher Blues' a day.

I spoke to a few other lads who were at school with me and now on day release from other factories in Belfast and, as we compared notes, I realised that I was quite well off working for Harland's. Some of the other guys told me that they had to go straight into the factory work. They had the most menial of tasks, their companies not having training facilities and they felt themselves lucky even to get day release. One of the boys Derek was a good friend and we came through school together until I went to Tech College. He stayed on at the Secondary School and then went to serve his time in a garage. He now was going to day release on a motor mechanics course.

'Come over to the sheds to see what I have,' he said

I followed him over to the bike shed and he stopped beside a motor- bike with L- plates taped to the front and back mudguards.

'What do you think of her?'

'Is she yours?' I whispered reverently.

'Yea, my Da bought it for me for getting to and from work, and I pay him back ten bob a week. Even with the cost of the petrol it is still cheaper than travelling on the train to work.'

I was astonished, Derek had only turned seventeen this year and here he was showing me his very own bike.

'How much did your Da pay for her?' I asked

'Twenty quid, and it is taxed till the end of the year. Do you want to start her up?'

'Can I?' I answered incredulously.

'Yes, turn the petrol on and tickle the carb a few times,' he instructed.

I had ridden old bikes over the fields across from our house with him for a couple of years. We had bought an old ex-GPO BSA Bantam from a scrap-man between four of us for five bob. Part of the fun was stripping it down and getting it to fire. My brother Robert was home from sea at the time and he taught us how to strip and clean the engine and carburettor. But Derek's bike was something else. It was a 175cc. James with headlight, speedo, (clocked up to 60 MPH!) a pillion seat, and she was gleaming like new. I was most impressed, how I longed to own such a bike.

She fired first push of the kick-start and I gave the throttle a few twists. We were covered in blue smoke and, as I breathed it in, the smell of the two-stroke oil exhaust, sent the hackles up on the back of my neck – nectar to the gods!

'She sounds beautiful,' I said, trying not to sound and look too jealous.

'You can have a shot round the school-yard after if you like,' he said generously.

'Dead on, I'll have to fly to the next class, but I will see you at four and take you up on that.' I shouted as I ran to the classroom.

We were given the programme of study and a class timetable after lunch and it didn't look too bad. We also were told the good news that the session ran from September until June each year, so we had the rest of the summer months off! I had covered most of the subjects whilst at school and felt I could handle the others. There was a big emphasis on mechanical drawing, mechanics, trig and metalwork, all these having double periods during the day, and one whole night of metalwork. This was now called workshop practice. The last class finished at four o'clock and I headed for the bike shed I saw Derek waiting for me, with the bike ticking over.

'What kept you? We were out ten minutes ago,' he said as I arrived breathlessly at the shed.

'Well, you know what old Scratch is like (aptly named as he was always scratching his nether regions), he works right to the bell. Is she warmed up?' I asked.

'Yes, off you go then, but not out of the yard as you are not insured for the main road.' This never stopped us before on the old bikes, but beggars can't be choosers, I thought.

I had a couple of laps of the playground, giving it big licks, but slowed down as the principle old Pete Gilchrist looked out of his window, and reluctantly handed the bike back to Derek.

'She is the deluxe model with the front and back lights and 6 volt battery,' Derek shouted as he strapped on his crash helmet.

He was starting to bore me a bit now, but I agreed with him that she was something else and arranged to see him later on in the week.

As I headed off home on the old pushbike I reflected on the day, musing that it wasn't all that bad being back at school, or day release as the teacher had rather grandly called it. I called into 'Woolies' and bought a few blocks of lined paper and some pens, as we had to supply our own stationery now we were working men.

Instead of having separate books for the different subjects, we were to use loose-leaf pads and file these in folders, which later proved easier to use for revision. I wondered why we didn't use these before at day school. Maybe it was too expensive compared with the standard issue of school exercise books.

'Had a good day son?' Ma said as I came up the front path to the house.

'Yes, very educational,' I replied sourly and she laughed.

'You are very lucky to get a day off work to go to school, and to get paid for it, none of the rest of the family got this chance, so make sure you take advantage of it.'

'Oh no!' I cried. 'I have forgotten to pick up my attendance card from the college; I will get hell from the Bowler in the morning.'

I jumped back onto the bike and pedalled off like mad towards the school, praying fervently that it hadn't yet closed for the day.

'You again? Sure where's the fire,' shouted the old janitor as I burst through the corridor doors.

'Is the office still open?' I bawled back at him.

'Aye if you hurry, the secretary usually works till five, what's up?' he croaked, choking on the dust or, the old pipe that stank of burned wood and was always clamped in his mouth, lit or otherwise.

'Forgot to pick up my day release card, I was at home when I remembered about it.'

'And what sort of a card is that,' he barked.

'Never mind, I will see you on the way out, but I can tell you this much, if I don't get it today, I am dead tomorrow,' I said as I left the old man in a wake of dust sweepings, tobacco smoke and bewilderment.

'Excuse me miss, do you have my day release card. I need it for work tomorrow?' I panted in a squeaky voice.

'Slow down there, aren't you Beth's wee brother?'

'Err, yes miss,' I replied.

'I have your card here, the principal has signed and I have stamped it up, I noticed it hadn't been picked up and I was going to give it to your Beth on the bus home. Don't you remember me? I used to come over to your house to see Beth and we would do our hair together,' she said in a rather posh voice.

'Oh yes!' I replied (I didn't like to tell her that Da said the house stank to high heavens for weeks after they had permed their hair in the back scullery.) 'Thanks very much, I am very grateful to you,' I said.

'No bother at all for a nice lad like you,' she smiled, 'You have really grown up quickly.'

I felt my face going red and rushed off back through the school corridors nearly knocking the janitor over again

'Get it then?' asked the janitor.

'Yes, have to go now,' I shouted as I flew through the doors into the schoolyard, being nearly run over by a lorry as I emerged from the yard onto the main road. I was too busy remembering the look on the secretary's face and her special smile that stayed with me all the way home. Maybe I was growing up, taking more notice of girls, but motorbikes, fishing and ships were still very much in my mind as I reached the front gate and cycled up the path.

My father had an old Norman Nippy moped. It had a small 50cc engine and pedals that were used to start it and assist it to climb up hills. I had been trying to pluck up the courage to ask him if I could learn to ride on it, once I was old enough to get a provisional motorcycle licence.

However as we all sat down to dinner, the talk was about a new order the aircraft factory had got, and 'Bank Line' had ordered another two cargo ships from the shipyard. Better than that, there was a letter from my brother, posted from Singapore. I wolfed down my spuds, boiled ham and cabbage then headed off up the stairs to read his letter and look up the atlas to see where Singapore was. I had marked out all the ports of call his ship had made and kept the stamps from his letters in a stamp album I had had for donkey's years.

He had told me on his last leave that this present ship was a tramp steamer, and was disgusted when I asked him if there were many tramps on board, and then he explained that the ship just went from one port to another depending on the cargo and had no set route. If he called at Japan he had promised to bring me home a new fishing rod, made from split bamboo cane whatever that was. The boys I went fishing with were very impressed when I told them about it.

I stayed in our room as I had homework to do; I thought I had seen the last of that! However here I was back at school and only a few weeks from my sixteenth birthday. The bedroom was shared with my three brothers, but I had the bed to myself when Robert was away at sea. My other two brothers had girlfriends (dolling or going strong as it was known) and were saving up to get married. They were out most nights till after 11'o'clock, and I was usually in the land of nod when they rolled in but sometimes I waited up for Johnny when I needed help with my homework. Other nights I would be awakened by one of my sisters hiding stockings or knickers from each other under my mattress, and then up would go the mattress again when one of them needed underwear again. However, getting back to the homework; this assignment wasn't too hard and I finished it off and got washed and ready to go out to BB.

Wednesday night was the first aid course and this proved to be time well spent in later years at sea. There were usually about fifteen boys at the course and we had a Red Cross instructor as well as an 'old boy'. An old boy was a BB lad who had passed through the BB into the old boys once he was eighteen. I had passed the elementary first aid examination and was due to sit the advanced course and hopefully get the first aid certificate and much-coveted badge.

I had earned several other badges; buglers, marching and wayfarers being among them and had been given a stripe and was a lance corporal, in charge of a team. (A 'Team Leader' in today's language.) The stripe was sewn onto a piece of black cloth and the badges pinned to the cloth. The cloth was attached to the upper arm with an elastic band and worn only on Friday night or special parades.) The course ended and we chatted in the hall for a while, putting away the stretcher and rolling up the bandages. I wandered up the road by myself. I called in at Toni's café as usual, for a coffee on the way home.

Now Toni was Italian and spoke with a very heavy accent; everything he said seemed to end in –aa, like what do you wanta tonighta? We used to take the mick out of him a bit, but it was all in good fun, his brother Sikee Tugnerie was a barber and had the shop next door to the café. His son Tug had been at the Tech with me.

'What you wanta tonighta Villie?'

'Coffee please, I'll take it over beside Derek'

'Want a lift up home Willie?' Derek asked.

'What about your L-plates, are you allowed to take me on the back?' I replied, sitting down.

'Should be okay at this time of night, but did you hear about the 'Q' cars?' he whispered out of the side of his mouth.

'What's that,' asked one of the bikers.

I was dumbfounded. None of the bikers had never looked in our direction before let alone spoken to us, and now all of a sudden they were all ears.

'Well,' explained Derek, 'my Da's in the B Specials, he says that there are Mini-Coopers with cops driving them and they follow along behind you and clock your speed. If you are over the speed limit they pull you over and book you for speeding.'

'Thanks' said the biker; looking over at his mates, 'we will have to look out for them. You had better not take your mate on the back until you pass your test, they will book you for it and take your mate's name as well. Do you want a lift on the back of my bike?' the biker asked looking at me.

'Me!' I spluttered, spilling half my coffee in the process. He must own one of the Triumphs or BSA machines parked outside Toni's. 'Yes please, I live just off the main Belfast Road.'

'That's okay we go home that way. I saw you looking at the bikes a few times, do you like bikes?'

'Not half, I work at the yard and am saving up for a bike – not like yours but a smaller one like Derek's.'

'What is yours, Derek?' he asked.

'175 James,' he said proudly.

'Nice wee machine, we all had to start somewhere; I passed my test on a 98cc James, and then had a 250 Biza for a while till I bought the Gold Star.'

'A Goldie! I've have seen these bikes racing at the Ulster Grand Prix at Dundrod and at the short circuit racing tracks at old air fields, but I have never been on one,' I answered excitedly.

'Well, now is your chance, I will drop you off on my way home, I live off the Shankill Road and work at the yard in the dry dock squad. I was a year in the Training Centre as well and I have two years done of my time as a fitter.'

My night was complete. As we headed for home I held onto his leather jacket for grim death, sliding backwards on the seat as he accelerated. The bike seemed to fly along the road and the sound was terrific. He dropped me off at the house and I introduced myself and asked him his name.

'George Smart,' he answered, 'I'll see you again at Toni's café and at the yard canteen if you like and you can meet some of the other lads who like bikes and racing.'

'Thanks a lot George, I really enjoyed the crack tonight in the café, and it was great to get a shot on the back of the Goldie, see you in work,' I shouted as he revved the bike up and took off up our hill with a roar and at a great rate of knots.

Granny Ferguson, who lived next door was looking out of her curtains as usual. She wasn't all that nosey I suppose, but liked to know what was going on in our street. She wasn't really our granny but we had called her that for as long as I can remember. Her husband (Granda Ferguson) had died a few years ago. He had worked as a riveter in the yard and had actually worked on the Titanic! He had told me a few good yarns about her, and I had listened all ears as he described the furniture and chandeliers, fitted to that ill-fated ship that had been built in Harland and Wolff and had sank on her maiden voyage in 1912.

He also explained to me how the 'heater', who heated the rivet on a coke brazier, threw it up to a 'catcher' who then passed it to the riveter, who inserted it in the hole and then, after alerting another riveter inside the hull, would start hammering. No wonder he was deaf as a post from this continual hammering of the rivets and plates.

I waved to Granny Ferguson as I walked up our path, but she just shook her head and closed over the curtain. I would probably get chapter and verse from my mother tomorrow, about hallions on motorbikes wakening up the neighbourhood. Mags was making up the pieces when I got into the house, Ma and Da were in bed and the rest of the tribe weren't in yet.

'How did you get on at first aid?' asked Mags.

'Oh all right, I am sitting the final exam in a few weeks, but you know what? I will have to give up PT and drill marching as I have night school Tuesday and Thursday nights now,' I replied.

'Oh well, at least you are getting a good education, we girls got nothing after we left school and, we left school when we were fourteen. By the way smarty pants, I start night school next Monday night!' she said excitedly. 'I am doing a twelve week cookery course and Ma and Da are helping with the course fees.'

'That's dead on! Will you be making buns and cakes and will you get to take them home?'

'Yes as far as I know, if they are cooked all right and are not burned, you can take them home.'

'I put a bit of ham left over from dinner in our pieces for tomorrow, do you want sauce on it?'

'Na, just as it is. The sauce soaks through the bread and makes it all mushy, but I still eat it. I am always starving at lunch break at work. I met a boy at Toni's tonight and he has a super bike, he gave me a lift home on his way to Belfast. He said he would meet me in the canteen tomorrow. I can't wait!'

'Just watch these Belfast people, I have known quite a few and some of them are all right but there is a lot of hard men as well, always fighting over religion or football'

'Don't worry; George is not like that he goes to the road races and dotes on his bike, and he wouldn't get into any bother like that. I am sending off for my provisional licence next month. It costs five bob and I need a photo for it, the photo is two bob alone.'

'I think we have a few of your old school photos from last year upstairs, we could cut your head and shoulders out of one of them and you could use that. I will have a look for you tomorrow.'

'Thanks Mags, I am off to bed. Do you think once I get my licence, Da would let me learn to ride on his wee bike?'

'I don't know, you could always ask him once your licence arrives,' she answered slowly. 'But don't get your hopes up too much; he really depends on the bike to get to work and the coastguards if he is called out!'

'See you tomorrow then. Old Granny Ferguson nearly fell out of her window tonight when I got off the back of George's bike.'

'Auch well, she is a poor old soul, but she always seems to be at the curtains when Dennis drives me home. He always waves at her and she jumps back and pulls the blind.' She laughed. Mags was going strong with Dennis; he had a black A40 Austin; registration MAD 40 (Margaret and Dennis)

So ended another day; day release and night school weren't so bad, the teachers were not as heavy handed and didn't bawl as much as normal day school. I found I really enjoyed a lot of the subjects, as I was starting putting them together with my new skills at work, so they now meant something to me.

I re-read Robert's letter before turning in, to dream of faraway places and of ships and tramps with their sooty faces and chimney brushes; looking over the rails waving at me to join them!

Chapter 3

BOYS' BRIGADE NIGHTS

The object of the Boys' Brigade is the advancement of Christ's kingdom among boys and the promotion of obedience, discipline, reverence and self- respect and all that lends itself to a Christian attitude.

'Squad! Squad; tallest to the right, shortest to the left, single rank file.' Roared the BB officer. 'By the right, number – odd numbers one pace back March! Form fours. By the left, in column of fours – quick march. Left right, left right, right wheel, Squ-aad Halt!'

'That was very good, boys,' praised Mr Brown, our Captain. 'We should do well in the competition.'

He was standing on the hall platform watching us being put through our paces for the Belfast Battalion Marching Competition that was to be held in Belfast in two weeks time. I quite enjoyed the marching and it helped with the band parades and contests. We had won the drill cup two years running and if we won this year we got to keep the cup.

'Squad dismiss,' Dennis Smith, the officer bawled. Then in normal tones congratulated us and said he was getting the silver polish out ready for the cup this year again.

'I have a bit of bad news, Dennis.'

'What's that, William?'

'I have night school twice a week now so I will have to give up the PT and drill marching. But don't worry; I will stay on for the contest.' I said, as he looked a bit crestfallen, this being so close to the contest.

'That's okay, the education always comes first, and you have done very well for us since you were about eleven years old.'

'Thanks for being so understanding Dennis. I have enjoyed every minute of the drill and PT and, it has kept me fit for the football matches. I'll really miss it.'

Although motorbikes, fishing and boats played a part in my teenage years, the BB took up a great part as well. Monday to Thursday I had bugle band, wayfarers (which also included map-reading and camping under canvas) marching, PT, and first aid. Friday night was parade; Saturday night was games night (football in the afternoon) and Sunday morning bible class.

Looking back the BB gave me a good grounding in the difference between right and wrong, and set the pattern for my love of camaraderie, which later followed on in the merchant navy and in Africa, as an ex-patriot engineer.

But my favourite BB night was Saturday night – games night! During the winter months, usually timed with the football season, the games would start at 7pm sharp. There was a league table formed by all the contestants – which was practically everyone in our company. The games were draughts, darts, billiards and table tennis. These games may seem a little dull by today's standards but we fought tooth and nail for every point. Two points were awarded for a win but none if you lost, and your opponent was awarded full points on your failure to turn up for the matches. Every one played against each other once a season.

The highlight of the evening was the undoubtedly the 'supper'. We were always starving! The officer's wives would make chips, beans and sausage rolls at about 9pm, by which time most of the games were over. We fairly wolfed this down and headed of home for 'match of the day' on the telly which started at 10pm.

We followed all the English first division teams' matches with great interest, cheering on Manchester United, Spurs and Liverpool. We had a special interest in Arsenal as Terry Neill had signed for them. Terry was an 'old boy' and I had played football with him when he was in the BB and old boys and he lived about 3 minutes from our house – my claim to fame! Then of course there was George Best, who played for Manchester United and the International team.

Terry returned from England regularly and led the Sunday morning bible class on a few occasions; his accent taking on a more pronounced English twang, every time he came home from across the water.

BB league football was played on Saturday morning or afternoon, depending on when we could book the local playing field. The team was announced at the close of Friday night parade and the places in the team were fiercely fought for. I played goalkeeper for many years, both for the BB and the Tech and am still paying for this with rickety knees! This came from breaking the ice in the goalmouth puddles in the frosty weather, and boy was the old leather ball heavy when wet; it felt a ton weight when I was taking goal kicks. In those days very few playing fields had changing rooms and showers, so we just washed in a nearby river or pulled our clothes over our skip – mud and all, risking the wrath of our mothers!

Another popular winter event was the pantomime. We put this on yearly and played to full houses for three nights. This added to our confidence – performing in front of an audience is quite nerve wrecking; especially when all the family and your mates are out front as well!

'Are you ready for the road Willie?' asked Nicky.

'Just about, are you for a coffee on the way home?' I asked as I put my uniform into my haversack. I had known Nicky (Nicolas) since school days; he was a very good footballer and was due to sign for our local Irish League team.

'How's working for a living agreeing with you Willie?' asked Nicky, as we sat down in Toni's café.

'Okay, better than being at school. I have a few good mates from Belfast and I have been in the Training School for 12 weeks, but it seems like 6 months. I can't wait to get out into the yard proper. We were allowed to see a launch of a ship last week, the place was packed and a real lady launched the ship with a bottle of champagne! Just like the movies.' I enthused.

'I'll give you a bit of advice Willie; – stick in there, I wish I could pass the entrance exam, but then I am not very scholarly, and I prefer to work outside anyway, but you have always liked old bikes and engines and things. I am hoping to get a start with Noel at your Da's work, could you put a good word in for me?'

'I thought you were turning professional,' I replied.

'No, it is just the amateur team so we get paid by a percentage of the gate at the match, not a wage as such.'

'Tell you what, why don't you send your Da up to our house and I will get my old man to see him?' I suggested.

We had our coffee and got the crack with a few mates, mostly about the football. I was proud to be a friend of Nicky's he knew a lot of good footballers and was a good mate of Terry Neill. I suppose he was right about the yard, it was just that I was so impatient and couldn't wait to be out in the real yard among the men!

We left the café and were walking up the road, when Archie Agnew, another one of the BB officers pulled in and offered us a lift in his car; an old A40.

'Hear you are off to the Irish League Nicky,' he said, changing up the gears with a crunch.

'Aye Archie. Willie is going to see his old man about a job on the building site for me. Bangor Football Club only pay you for the Saturday afternoon, and maybe a bonus if we play the Blues at Windsor.'

The Blues were Linfield Club, from Belfast and they were usually Irish League and Ulster cup winners every year, and had a big protestant following. They played at Windsor Park, where the Northern Ireland International team played matches against England, Scotland and Wales. These were known as the 'Home Internationals' and I seldom missed a chance to see our team in action.

'Well Willie, what about you? How's the old shipyard treating you?' asked Archie.

'Oh dead on, I really enjoy my job and I will soon be moving from the bench fitting to the machining area. We are making our own tools!'

I said proudly.

'Well that is good, I am sure you will do well, have you heard from Robert?'

'Aye, I had a letter last week, he was in Burma at a place called Rangoon, but only for a few days then his ship is off to Japan!'

'You sound like you can't wait to join the navy Willie, but take your time. Enjoy the next few years – they are the best years of your life. Just remember what you learned whilst in the BB and remember, if it doesn't feel right; don't do it. No matter where you are in the world, you won't go too far wrong.'

I still remember that conversation with Archie Agnew as if it were yesterday, and it was very sound advice for me – a sixteen year old boy slowly turning into a man, on the first rung of my chosen career.

Chapter 4

LOOK BEFORE YOU LEAP

'It is getting darker in the morning' said James, stifling a yawn.

'It sure is, and harder to get out of bed! I replied. I wish it was the summer and I was off to BB camp in Scotland.'

We were on the early morning train to Belfast. I had only met James a few weeks ago. He had moved to Bangor recently and lived only a few streets from our house. He was very quietly spoken, so I was surprised at him starting the conversation.

We got off the train together at Ballymacarrot Halt, which I had found was nearer the Training School than the main Belfast station.

'I am moving onto the deep water berth today,' said James. There is a Bank boat just off the slips and I am running electricity to the temporary lights. James was an apprentice electrician and had done two years of his time. The deep-water berth was where the ships came alongside to be fitted out. The engines were my main interest so I asked James to let me know when they were to be fitted.

'I will keep an eye out for them coming from the engine works, but I am down in the holds most of the times. I am looking forward to the cabins and bridge getting wired up, it will be a lot of work and we may get overtime.'

'What's overtime?' I asked

'Well you know we work from eight till five during the week?' I nodded.

'Anytime after these hours is overtime and you get paid extra for it, but the gaffers don't like having to work overtime as it puts more cost on the job; so less profit for the managers. We might be asked to work part of the Christmas holidays.

'I don't fancy any of that; I find I am knackered after a normal shift, let alone working longer. By the time I get home and washed it is coming up to seven and I am off to night school or the BB's. I am looking forward to a few days off at Christmas.'

We walked on in silence for a while then I came to the training centre entrance doors.

'See you on the way home,' I called to James.

'Houl on a wee minute. If you come to the end of the road, I will show you the ship I am working on.'

'Okay,' I replied as we walked towards the deep water, or I assumed so, as I could see a few ships tied up in the distance.

'That's my ship, the one with the tugs alongside still.'

'Why! Would you look at the size of that! It's enormous,' I yelled, causing a few of the men to look back and laugh.

'It just looks that big as it is so far out of the water,' said James. 'Once the engines are in her and all the accommodation and cargo she will sink down a bit.'

'Well I think she looks swell as she is, how I wish I was working out here instead of the training school,' I said wistfully.

'Take your time, there is lots to learn before you get out here, sometimes I wish I was back in the training school, it is very hard work out here and everyone takes a hand out of you. You never know when they are serious.'

'I'm off – see you on the train,' I shouted as I ran back down the road, making hard going of it, as everyone else seemed to be going the other way.

I clocked in dead on eight, under the watchful eye of Mr Fullerton, the bowler.

'Just made it Scott, sleep in?'

'No,' I replied. 'I was over at the deep water looking at the Bank boat, my mate is an apprentice electrician on her.' 'Do we ever get out seeing a ship fitting out? Have you ever been in that squad?'

'Doubtful to the first question and yes I was a foreman fitter, in the outfitting squad before coming to the school.' He replied. 'Get into your overalls and I'll see you at the bench.'

'Right lads, gather round, I want a word with you all.'

'Sounds ominous,' whispered one of the boys with a grin, 'something in the wind.'

'Quietly now, settle down,' said Mr Fullerton. 'We will be cracking on with making your own tools for a few weeks and today we are going to be working at the forge. I will show you how to harden and temper the jaws for you pipe wrenches and mole grips. Remember the film about this?' What is the reason for hardening, then tempering – Scott, lets see if you have been awake during the lecture!'

'Yes sir, hardening is so that the teeth won't wear out and tempering is used to prevent the teeth from breaking or cracking,' I replied confidently.

'Near enough, I suppose – must have been your mate snoring!' he said grinning. 'Does anyone remember the colours for hardening and tempering? – Not you Scott, don't push your luck,' he winked. 'Barlow! How about you?'

'Red for hardening and black for tempering,' Jamsey replied.

'No – anyone else? You Nickle?'

'I, ah, – red for hardening, straw brown for tempering,' offered Nicks.

'Not bad; let's see how we go at the real thing,' he said, leading us up to the forges.

We were the only ones at the forges, and as there were four of them, we paired off – two of us per unit. The forges were set ready to start and after donning asbestos gauntlets, the bowler showed us how to light the gas 'poker' and push it well into the coke, to get the fire started. Once we were all fired up and the coke glowing red, we gripped the jaws to be heat-treated in long handled tongs and thrust them into the glowing embers.

We quenched them in the water buckets as the colours changed, completing the hardening and tempering process. It was hot work and after we had all completed the tasks, we raked over the cinders and let the fires die down, as it was nearly lunchtime.

The hooter blew and we all took off for the canteen. As I joined the queue, a big rough git (our wee English teacher would have called him a lout!) pushed into the line, causing a minor ruckus as we all backed onto our neighbour's toes.

'Watch it you big eejit!' I shouted at him.

'What are you going to do about it? Who are you calling an eejit?' replied Loutie.

This brought loud jeers and cries of derision from the rest of the lads in the queue.

'I was only saying to take your time – there's plenty for all'.

'Well, I don't like your attitude, keep out of my way, if you know what's good for you,' he spouted.

Louder jeers this time along with two - toned oo's

I was beetroot by this time but being overawed, or chicken or both, I let it go and carried up the line towards the canteen ladies.

'Mug of tea and a custard tart please?' I requested.

'Sure, want milk and sugar in your tea son?'

'Yes please.

'Nice to see some folk have manners,' she answered looking pointedly in the louts' direction.

I walked over to our usual table and loutie was sitting at it.

'No hard feelings Bangor,' he said offering me his hand, (it was usual to be called by your home town, if you didn't come from Belfast). 'Didn't know you were an old hand of George, and you did sort out that Grand Masters boy last week. Wish I had seen it. Hear you are into bikes?'

'Yea' I answered cautiously taking his outstretched hand, 'I get to most of the races and am after a bike of my own.'

We chatted for a while and then headed back to the training school.

The horn blew as we ran into the training school. We were back on the bench this afternoon, finishing off our engineer's squares. These were made up from two pieces of tool steel comprising of a handle and blade, riveted at exactly 90 degrees to each other. I had almost finished mine and had signed out the Moore and Wright 'master square' to check if I had got the angle of mine right.

This was done initially by holding the master against my own square. Engineer's blue was smeared onto the master blade. The blue rubbed off onto my square, showing high spots that would be draw filed until a continuous line of marking blue appeared on my square. I had just carried out the final checking and had put my square into the vice to lightly file away the last wee high spot.

'Fancy a fag in the bogs, Willie?' asked Nicks, 'I am fair fed up with this filing lark!

'Aye all right, could do with one.' 'You go first and I will follow you on.'

We weren't allowed to smoke at the training centre, so we would slope off for a sly puff in the bogs. We had a few drags each from the same butt and headed back down to the benches. (You couldn't stay away too long as bowler would regularly 'raid' the bogs)

'There's "head the balls" mate walking away from our bench,' said Nicks, pointing down the workshop. 'He's a shipwright and shouldn't be on our side of the shop.'

'Who's head the ball?'

'You know; yer man – that git you almost stuck one on in the canteen at lunchtime'

'Oh him, that tube.'

I walked over to the bench and started filing the blade of the square. I happened to look along the handle and nearly passed out; the handle had a M & W stamp on it, and here was me – filing away at it.

I had a quick look round and spotted a head looking in my direction from over the dividing wall and a hand appeared along with it, giving me the fingers! It was the shipwright we had seen sneaking around our bench. He must have swopped the squares around in the vice, obviously to get back at me for having a go at his mate in the canteen – Nicks was right!

I removed the square from the vice. Luckily, I had seen the stamp before I had done any permanent damage to the accuracy of the master; and I was using copper vice grips, nevertheless I went up to the bowler;

'Can I see you for a wee minute Mr Fullerton,' I asked nervously.

'All right, come into the office.'

'You know the way we are making our own tools.'

'Yes – get on with it!' Spit it out, I saw you looking sheepish back there,' he said pointing to the workbench.

By this time all the boys were looking at me in the office, but feigning any interest in the proceedings. Dear God knows what they thought was going on, as I had spoken to no one before the gaffer.

'Well, I was marking off my square against the master, and put the master in the vice by mistake; I filed a wee bit off the blade before I realised my mistake.'

'And why are you telling me all this, I would never have known, or did you think I saw you?'

'No, no indeed not! it was just that it is the master and everyone depends on it to be square, but now it might be a bit off, so everyone else's would be wrong as well.'

'Right Scott – into the head instructors' office, wait now.' He looked back at the workbenches, 'what are all yous looking at, no work to do? I'll soon fix that,' he bawled at my mates and pushed me ahead of him towards the manager's office. He knocked on the glass door.

'Come in,' a voice in muffled tone came through the glass.

'This is Scott Mr Cummings,' the gaffer started.

'Yes I know him, started a row in the canteen a few weeks ago with Malcolm's son, mind you that wouldn't be hard, Malcolm himself is not the easiest to get on with at the best of times. You remember him, when he was working on the slips Michael?'

'Don't I just, a right hard man – always had to be right?' replied my gaffer, half shutting his eyes.

35

'Well Scott, have you been fighting again?'

'No Mr Cummings,' I said, trying not to look at his big, really big red nose with caverns in it. 'I was making a square…

'I will tell the chief what you did Scott,' said the gaffer, and proceeded to give him chapter and verse.

I was expecting the worse – suspension or bagged. Imagine the shame of it all! Oh aye him – lasted three months, couldn't stick the pace. I could hear them all now.

'Right Scott – wait outside and close the door after you.'

They called me in after a few minutes, and both looked very stern. Aye well, I thought, enjoyed it while it lasted.

'We have decided to let you off with a verbal warning this time! What you did was wrong, but because you owned up to it, there is no real harm done. If you had kept quiet, a lot of damage could have been done. These tools you are making are for life, and, as you realised, they have to be accurate. I will send the master square over to the tool room and have it checked. Now get back to work,' said Mr Cummings with a severe voice, 'we will be keeping an eye on you in future, and hold that temper in check.'

Well, I took off like a bat out of hell, nearly tripping over the gaffer and headed for my bench.

'What was all that about,' asked Nicks.

'I'll tell you later, I made a balls-up with the M & W square, and had to tell them. Do you know what? They knew about my row in the canteen; but for some reason, I got away with it.'

I had learned my lesson, always double check before starting to file? Well yes, but more importantly, admit mistakes right away and be prepared to take the consequences. It is hard at the time but invariably is the best way

Chapter 5

BOATS AND RODS

Big Noel and I did most of our fishing from White Rock, a large rock on the coast-line below the golf course at Carnalea on the shores of Belfast Lough. We caught whiting, blocken also known as coalfish, gurnard, lithe, and mackerel in season. We also went after dogfish and Frankie my eldest brother had fashioned a pater-noster type trace from piano wire. I attached this to the end of my line and this stopped the dogfish biting through it. They were very hard to get off the hook once they were landed, as they had very sharp teeth, like a baby shark. They also had a spur of bone sticking out of their tail, which could impale the unwary and leave a nasty slash on the arm or wrist.

However, we only fished for doggies when there wasn't anything else around, and of course we couldn't eat them, or so we thought until a few years back. I had been to Cleethorpes in England on BB camp, and lo and behold; dogfish were on sale in the fish and chip shops, as battered rock cod! Yucht!

The mackerel were great crack, giving a lively fight when we were using fine catgut and light rods. We made our rods from ordinary bamboo canes, bought in the local gardening shop. A top eye was screwed into the top and glued in (I used Frankie's horse-hoof glue, which he used on piano innards and smelt terrible when boiling on the gas cooker) and several other eyes lashed onto the cane at regular intervals.

Fishing line, not gut, was wound round the other end and this when varnished, served as the handle. A bakelite fixed spool reel was lashed to the handle and then the completed rod was given another couple of coats of varnish, and left to dry out for a few days. We used about six pounds breaking strain cat-gut and a plastic float, set at whatever depth we thought the fish where feeding. The rods got broken regularly, but only cost a few pence to put right.

'See the birds over there, beside that clump of weed,' hissed Noel out of the side of his mouth.

'Aye, they are dipping for fry, looks like we are in for a shoal of mackerel,' I answered, never taking my eye of my float.

I was right; down went Noel's float followed by mine, both of us striking simultaneously.

'Got one on, it feels like a beauty,'

'Me too,' I shouted, there must be stacks of them coming in.

We reeled them in and re-cast with new bait, although my Da use to say that when the mackerel were running after the herring fry like this, they would jump onto the bare hooks!

'That will do me for the night,' said Noel threading a piece of string through the mackerel's gills and making a loop to carry them.

'Aye me as well, I have about a dozen good ones and a couple of small ones for bait. My Uncle Jimmy will want a few for the pots. Are you coming down to see him with me, he'll have the boat tied up at the pier, or the Hole?'

'No, not the night, I promised old Granny Ferguson I would plaster her back yard, you should see it! Hasn't seen a lick of whitewash in donkeys' years so I'll give it a few coats after I plaster it.'

Uncle Jimmy had a boat that he used to take people out fishing, and pleasure cruises along Belfast Lough. He used to share a deep sea fishing boat and along with my Granda, Da and his other brother, fishing for the herring in the Irish sea and across in Scottish waters, till the herring got scarce. He also had about 30 skiffs and punts that he hired out in the summer. I had worked on these for him for years, whilst at school. I got burned almost black in the summer and became a strong rower, and, more importantly, getting to know the different moods of the sea.

I headed on along the shore footpath, past Picky Pool; the outdoor swimming pool and on along the promenade, past the three piers until I came to the Long Hole. This was a small harbour, bound to seaward by rocks, and landward by a sea wall built between the hole and the Seacliff Road. I tried here first as sometimes he kept the boat tied up in the small harbour.

Sure enough, Uncle Jimmy was sitting mending pots on the sea wall. I can't remember him being young or getting older, he seemed to stay the same age. As usual he was wearing his captains hat, an old fisherman's' jersey and faded blue bib and tucker overalls, over which were his sea-boots, rolled down to calf height. He looked up as I sat down beside him.

'Had a good catch?'

'Yes, I will take a few home for our supper and you can have the rest, are you going out tonight,' I asked, looking out to sea.

'No, but I will be needing a hand on Saturday morning, bright and early mind, no later than half past three!' I am taking a few big nobs out to the Copeland Islands on a fishing trip. They are from London and staying at the Royal Hotel.' He took the pipe out of his mouth and spat accurately into the water of the Hole.

Must be very rich, I thought, the Royal Hotel stood on the esplanade and, by all accounts was a very expensive place to stay.

'I'll be here, I have no football on Saturday, but I am going out with a friend later on in the afternoon. We are going shooting, for wood pigeons, and afterwards dig in for the evening flight of ducks. He got a new gun - a five shot automatic repeater. I bought his single barrel of him for three quid. It is a BSA Snipe; 12 bore, full choke, 30 inch, hammerless with ejector.' I finished breathlessly.

'Don't go much for these new fangled repeater shotguns, if you can't hit it with a double barrel, hardly worth using five shots, is it?'

'No, I suppose not. Have you still got your old double?' I asked tentatively, he guarded this gun with great zeal. It was a Spanish hammer gun, with engraving along the breech and carvings on the wooden stock, but I never saw it off his fireplace wall. However, I can remember him coming up to our house for a bath, when I was a nipper, and giving Ma a few rabbits he had shot. When I was younger, I gave these dead bunnies a very wide berth!

He spat into the sea and ignored me, so I let it go. Robert had asked for a look at his shotgun one time, actually reaching up to the fireplace to touch it. He got a right rollicking and nearly had his head tore off by Uncle Jimmy. He just wouldn't let anyone near it. Maybe I would get the story someday.

'Want to pump her out for me; she is due an overhaul this winter. I'll get her pulled up the slip, and see where the leaks are?' he said, looking down towards the boat.

'Sure thing,' I answered, jumping from the sea wall to the deck of his boat. It was about twenty foot long, eight foot wide with a cabin for'ard. She had an inboard diesel engine in the centre, which was covered in a tin cowling. I loved to sit on this cowling when we were in Belfast Lough fishing, as it was always nice and warm on my backside.

I unscrewed the bilge pump overboard outlet and started pumping, moving the handle backwards and forwards watching the spout of oily bilge water cascade into the water of the Hole. I pumped her dry, replaced the plug in the pump outlet and climbed up to the wall again.

'How's your Ma and Da boy?' he never called me William, except when I had done something stupid, like throwing a pot over the side, without checking if it was baited first, or dropping live a pot back into the sea.

'Dead on,' I replied.

'Is this the shipyard language? What's it like up there now? Many men working?'

'Aye, plenty of work, I'll be out of the training school soon, and I will be working out in the yard.'

He spat again, 'head-cases the lot of them if you ask me; always striking, and for what? a halfpenny extra an hour!'

I could tell he was off again, so I told him I had to go home, and that I would be down at 3 am on Saturday morning to pump out the bilges and warm up the diesel engine. She was a pig to start, but Uncle Jimmy had the knack of it and had shown me. The trick was to lift the de-compressors on the cylinder heads, get it up to the compression stroke and swing like mad, dropping the de-compressors at exactly the right moment.

It was also very important not to hold the starting handle in a full grip, only partial grip, as if the engine backfired, the handle swung violently in the opposite direction, breaking your wrist in the process! This was very good training for me, as in later years at sea; I was in charge the lifeboats and fire pumps; all having diesel engines and started by swinging the starting handle.

I got home about eight and cleaned and salted the fish. Da put the pan on and we had a good tasty supper of mackerel and soda-bread and butter, with lashings of tea. No one could fry fish like my Da, he got them just right, crispy on the outside and just moist in the middle. I shouted to Noel, who was finishing of Granny Ferguson's yard next door, and he joined us as well.

'Doing a homer big Noel,' said Da. 'Hope you are fit for tomorrow; we have a big job on at the Palace Barracks in Hollywood. The Sherwood Forrester's regiment is due across in a few months and the MOD wants all the houses and barracks done up, ready by then.'

'No problem Mr Scott, I was just helping Granny to tidy up her yard – an hours work and I'm done. I'll give it a couple of coats of whitewash at the weekend. These fish are dead on!' said the big man, delving into the fried mackerel.

'Don't forget we are going shooting on Saturday afternoon. I got my new Firearms Certificate yesterday, so I am all legal.' I said to Noel through a mouthful of fish. I had had to go down to the local police barracks to apply for the certificate; but had no trouble as my Da knew Sergeant Rankin; the Police Station Sergeant

I saw Noel to the door and walked up the back path with him and tackled him as he jumped the garden fence between Granny Ferguson's and us.

'Will you lend me a few cartridges on Saturday? I am broke this week, but I will give them back to you next week?' I pleaded.

'I will give you a dozen of my old ones; you can have them for nothing. The ones I use are especially for the five shot; they are not supposed to jam, like the cheap ones.'

'Dead on! I am away with my Uncle Jimmy early on Saturday, but I will be back for about two so as to catch the tide in the Hole, so I will call for you at about half past.'

'That's fine; I am working on Saturday morning anyhow with your Da at the Barracks. Do you know there is a big barbed-wire fence right around the barracks, and machine gun posts at the main gates?' he said.

'I heard that, we pass there in the train on the way to the yard, but it is too far away to see the gates. Anyhow it's nothing to do with us; the soldiers just go around Belfast and Derry not here in Bangor; thank goodness.'

'Yes, but the troubles are starting again, my Da said it was like this before the last time; everyone ended up fighting in a civil war!' he answered.

I didn't know what he meant, so I changed the subject, telling him about Uncle Jimmy's shotgun. Noel agreed that it was a bit strange, but said it was his gun to do with as liked.

'Are you still going to the BBs?' asked Noel.

'Aye, not so much now, I have the Tech two nights a week, so I only go to band and Parade nights, the games nights are finished 'till the winter again. I will probably pack it in next year, after camp. We are going to Aberfoyle, in Scotland this year and it's under canvas. I quite fancy that - up in the highlands with all the kilties!'

'See you Saturday,' I said to Noel as I locked our back gate and headed into the house.

Mags was doing the dishes and I gave her a hand.

'Those fish were lovely and tasty William, did you get them off the pier?'

'No; down at the rocks at Bangor West, below Carnalea Golf Links. There were stacks of mackerel, but they don't keep, so I gave a few to Uncle Jimmy for the pots. I am going out on Saturday with him dead early, can you lend me your alarm so I don't sleep in, you know what he is like, if you are not on time?'

'Yes sure, remind me before I go out on Friday night. Did you see wee Jean's catalogue; there is a Dansette record player in it for four pounds ten. (Jean was Johnny's girlfriend, and they were saving up to get married) It is electric and holds about six records and keeps playing, so you don't have to keep getting up and changing the records. Do you want to go halfers with me for it, it will cost us a shilling a week each to pay it off?'

'Sounds good to me, order it up and we will buy it between us,' I replied.

We all used Da's old polished wood HMV record player. It had a handle at the side for winding it up, but this would suddenly unwind, as there was something wrong with the spring mechanism, so we had to put a couple of hefty books on the handle after winding it up. It played 78s and 33s but the new records coming out were 45s and this is why Mags was after the Dansette.

'I am off to bed. Lie in till eight-tomorrow morning as I have day release, night, night, Mags.'

Photograph of me in our back garden about 1963; with a few mackerel for supper and my new split cane rod Robert brought me back from Japan.

'Night child, see you tomorrow,' answered Mags.

The rest of the week passed without any further incidents and Saturday came at last! I had been up since 2.30am, made my way down to the pier and was now on board 'Maggie'; Uncle Jimmy had moved her from the Hole and tied her up at the pier. I had come down early to pump out the bilges and warm her up. I finished pumping her out and looked up to see him coming along the pier with a bucket of bait. I would recognise that gait anywhere; he rolled rather than walked, and always had the old pipe going on some sort of 'black twist' tobacco.

I checked the fuel tank and oil sump and turned the engine over a few times, before de-compressing the head and firing her up. She coughed into life, and I pulled the throttle, I loved the sound of the exhaust burbling into the sea, the smell of the nets, tar, and overall the tangy smell of the misty sea.

'Here all night?' he greeted me.

'Good morning to you too, I got up early to get her ready, Da says to ask you to give him a few cod up home, if we have plenty,' I said.

'Looks a good day for it, be light afore long, give her a kick ahead and astern boy, but don't strain the ropes.'

Soon our passengers arrived and I gave them a hand to board. They were English and had very posh accents. What an assortment of fancy rods and reels they had. The rods were heavy cane and tubular steel, and the reels were large fixed spools. Both rods and reels had brass fittings, and shone like gold in the early morning light.

Uncle Jimmy took her out as I cast off from the pier bollards and jumped back aboard.

I sat down beside the Englishmen. There were very friendly and offered us coffee from their thermos flasks and fancy English fags about six inches long. The coffee tasted great and warmed us up. As the sun came up there was a slight swell, and I was explaining to the men where we were going to fish.

'Should get a few good cod, but watch out for the conger eels, they are nasty and it's better to cut the line and let them off rather than bring them into the boat.

'Why is that Mate?' one of them twanged.

'Well you see Mr Connors; they have very sharp teeth pointing backwards and strong jaws, we took one aboard a few weeks ago. It was about ten feet long, and it bit right through one of the fisherman's boot and took off half his big toe! What a mess the boat was in. They both looked at me as if I was mad but Uncle Jimmy spat overboard and told them it was true.

They still looked unconvinced, but we were coming up to our fishing spot, and as the boat slowed down I went up to the bows and threw the anchor over. Uncle Jimmy went astern and then cut the engine.

'Well gents, get after them, there's rag worm, mackerel or herring for bait so you have a choice.'

We caught a boatload of cod, flatfish and skate (a fish like a small sting-ray – only the wings were kept, the bodies were thrown overboard) and a few mackerel, so the English men were very pleased, even though they didn't get any congers.

We could see quite a crowd of people on the pier. Uncle Jimmy turned to me,

'Take her in boy, steady mind you. Pay no attention to that lot on the pier; they only want to see what we caught.'

This was the first time he had let me bring the boat alongside and I was very nervous, but I had handled her in the Hole and taken her out from the pier. I cut the revs and put her in neutral then slow astern; gently we nudged against the wooden sides of the pier with hardly a shudder. Uncle Jimmy jumped onto the pier with the mooring rope and helped the passengers ashore.

We tied up and the Englishmen said goodbye and thanked us for the best day of fishing – ever.

That's for you, he said handing me a ten bob note! I looked over at Uncle Jimmy. 'He has been paid; that's for you, we'll be back next year and will look you up.'

'Thanks, it has been a pleasure, I look forward to seeing you all again', I said excitedly, not believing my eyes.

'You did well, boy,' said Uncle Jimmy, nice bit of boat handling, and he gave me another ten bob note! I was rich! 'Pick a couple of cod out for your Da, and tell him I will see him at the Coastguards practice tonight.'

Chapter 6

A BIT OF ROUGH SHOOTING

After I left Uncle Jimmy, I ran along the pier, onto the bike, and pedalled like mad up home, gave the fish to Ma and told her I was away shooting with Noel. I met Noel and he gave me a handful of cartridges. I told him about the morning as we walked up the road, with the guns under our arms, and his dog at our heels.

'I bought a few pigeon decoys from the sports shop on my way from work,' said Noel, 'they should help us pull a few birds down to range.'

Now the woodies were a very wary bird, they could spot your face a mile away, so you had to be dug-in well and keep you face covered. We put the decoys out on a field of barley stubble. We had permission to shoot over a lot of farmer's ground as we kept the pigeons and crows, on the move. We missed a lot, but managed to shoot a few as well!

'Down Noel,' I whispered, 'flock of woodies coming in against the wind and circling towards the decoys.'

'You have first crack Willie, and I will open up at them on the way out.'

Not daft big man I thought, as they were easier to hit when flying away from you. Bang! I pulled the leading two down and then Noel opened up with the five shot... Bang! Bang! Bang! Bang...

'Got three,' shouted Noel. 'Come on Willie! Run! One of yours is just winged.'

Sure enough, I had shot one stone dead, but the other was winged. I ran across and wrung its' neck, setting the two of them up beside the other decoys, facing into the wind, with a few twigs under their necks to hold their heads up. This made them more realistic. (According to the Shooting Times Magazine) Noel did the same, so we had plenty of decoys out now, and this brought even more birds down to us.

'I am for a drop of tea,' said big Noel as he brought out his flask. I was going to buy a flask as soon as I could afford it. I used an old lemonade bottle filled with tea and it worked okay in the summer, but went cold very quick in the winter.

We sat together and discussed the possibilities of the night flight of ducks. They normally fed on barley stubble and liked it better when there was a bit of rainwater lying in puddles.

'Did you see thawn daft dog of mine, nearly plucked the bloody pigeons, the way it was retrieving them. Shook them to bits, I don't think she'll do Willie?'

'Oh well; sure Chep is good as gold, sitting here. When I miss a bird she looks up in disgust you know,' I laughed, 'she will come all right, give her time.'

We dug in beside a partially flooded barley field, which was on the duck - flight path to the local Ballysallagh Reservoirs, and waited. It was almost dark and I just saw the outline of a duck about 50 yards away, coming into land on the field. Bang! I let fly, followed by another four shots from Noel and we ran into the field with Chep going off its head completely, not knowing which way to turn.

'Got a drake,' I shouted excitedly.

'Got three out of four Willie,' replied Noel shakily, 'that was some shot of yours Willie, my three were overhead.'

We gathered up the ducks and as it was pitch black, started off for home.

'Did I tell you that your man Jimmy the chef, who plays football with us, was asking about woodies and ducks. He said that the manager of the Crawfordsburn Inn would buy some of us?'

'Lets go and see him now, it's on our way home,' I replied.

We went to the back door of the Inn and asked for Jimmy McLaughlin, the chef. Jimmy came out in his working gear of white top and black and white checked trousers, he was sweating buckets.

'Fit like boys,' he asked in his queer Scottish accent. He hailed from Aberdeen. 'I am fair gasping,' he said as he lit a fag.

'We were wondering if you could do with some woodies and a few mallard.' Noel asked.

'Stay right there, I'll be right back the noo' he said handing me his fag and disappearing through the door. He came back with the manager.

'Lets have a look at the birds,' he said, looking at Noel and I suspiciously, 'I don't want them if they are full of shot!'

'Och Naw boss; they boys are fine sports and would have shot them at a good distance,' answered Jimmy on our behalf. (If the birds were shot at close range, there would have been a lot of lead shot in them.)

'What were they feeding on,' asked Jimmy's boss.

'Barley stubble and grass,' Noel answered quickly, before I could utter a word. 'Well, these look okay; I will give you a bob each for the pigeons and three and a tanner, for the mallard.'

I let him have four woodies. I wasn't parting with my other three woodies or the duck. That was our Sunday dinner!

'Come into the bar and I will stand you a drink,' the manager said.

So we ended up in the public bar, guns, Chep and all. He stood us a Guinness apiece and I tasted my first bottle of stout. I hoped there was no one we knew in the bar, but it looked quite posh, so I thought we were safe. I shudder to think what Ma and Da would say if they thought I had started drinking!

'Why did you answer yer man so quickly when he asked what the ducks had been feeding on Noel,' I asked as I drank the bitter tasting Guinness, spitting out a piece of cork.

'Jimmy told me a while ago they paid more for ducks feeding inshore than one feeding on the foreshore, on seaweed, mussels and worms; 'probably tasted better, when they had been feeding on barley!'

We walked down the road on air; I had made a good few bob today, from fishing and shooting, and really enjoyed myself into the bargain.

'You are very quiet Willie, what's up?'

'Oh nothing, I am just tired I have been up since two this morning and was thinking of my bed, but I will have to clean and pluck the duck and a couple of woodies before I turn in.'

'Well, you have a lie in tomorrow, it's Sunday,'

'Right enough; I have bible class at ten. I will give church a miss, and do a bit of work on my Da's bike, it needs a de-coke badly, he says there is no power in it.'

'Did you ask him about the L-plates?'

'Yes, he says I can learn on the bike once the licence comes through, I applied six weeks ago, you know!'

'Ach, sure these things take time, remember it has to come from Downpatrick; my Provisional Car Licence took six weeks.' Noel was learning to drive in Sean's car; his sister Hazel's boyfriend.

'Yes, shouldn't be much longer, I am not half looking forward to getting out on the road.' I said wistfully.

We said goodnight at our back gate and I hung the duck and pigeons up on a nail in the coalhouse and went inside.

Boy was I looking forward to bed. Da was just in from the coastguards and I told him that I had shot a duck at last.

'That will do nicely for tomorrow's lunch, I saw your Uncle Jimmy at coastguard practice and he said you did well today. Brought the Maggie alongside yourself he tells me. Ma has kept a bit of cod warm for your supper, then bed for you! I'll see to the birds.'

'Yes,' I replied,' we had a great morning out on the boat, he is a great sailor you know, has a nose for the fish.'

'Hey! Hold on there! Sure wasn't I at sea with him for years? The other boats used to follow us as Jimmy could always find the herring.'

I had my supper and a quick wash at the sink, 'Night all, I am off to bed, will you call me at nine for bible class Da?'

'Yes, night son, see you in the morning; and well done!'

Chapter 7

ON THE ROAD AT LAST

It was 11 o'clock, the next morning and I had just got back from bible class. Every-one else was at church and I was in the shed stripping down Da's 50cc Norman Nippy, as it was going too well. I had taken out the spark plug and gave it a good clean up. I set the gap using a piece of Park-Drive fag packet, and set it aside. I took of the four cylinder head bolts and lifted off the wee cylinder head. No wonder it was sick! There was a big build-up of carbon on the head and piston crown.

I scraped off the carbon from the top of the piston, with a penny, being careful not to let any dirt fall down the barrel. I put the head onto an old wooden bench that a neighbour, Mr Thompson had built for us, along with the shed. He was a joiner and lived a few doors away.

I cleaned the carbon off the head, with the same penny, (Robert had told me to use a penny as the copper didn't score the aluminium head or piston) and then washed it in paraffin before re-assembling the engine. I then unclamped the silencer, stripped out the baffles, and washed them in paraffin as these too were choked solid. After bolting up the silencer again, I switched the petrol on, and pedalled like mad. At last she fired and immediately the shed was covered in two-stroke exhaust fumes, but I didn't mind this at all and just opened the shed door to let them out.

I sat on the bike seat and taking it off the stand, backed her out of the shed and took her up the back path for a spin. It had two gears and a clutch, operated from the left handle bar, and the front brake and throttle on the right side. Pedalling backwards operated the back brake.

'What's all that racket?' shouted Da, over the noise of the engine.

'I have de-coked her and boy was she needing it,' I shouted back.

I cut the engine and put her on the stand. 'I'll polish her up now and she will be like a new bike tomorrow.'

'Hope you screwed the plug in all right,' said Da.

'Yes, on the right threads and good and tight. (In some far and distant past, Da had owned on old Plymouth car when he lived in Canada, and a mechanic had cross-threaded the plugs. He had to get a new cylinder head and had never forgotten this!)

I put the bike back on the stand and went into the house to get the Brillo pads and Brasso, and bumped into Ma and the sisters, just back from church.

'Teapot on William, why weren't you at church today?'

'Aw Ma, give over, I was at bible class then came home to do Da's bike, it was on it's last legs.'

'Oh no,' exclaimed Ma, 'I forgot to tell you there was a letter for you last week and I put it behind the clock, I think it might be your licence William.'

I ran into the living room and leaned over the hearth to the clock. I sifted through the letters, (all the mail ended up behind the clock, and it gradually edged its way towards the front of the wooden mantle piece) sure enough there was a brown envelope with my name on it; Master William Scott, Master indeed!

I opened it up and there was my provisional licence. It was green and had my ugly mug on the inside. I was licensed to drive a motorcycle – at last!

'Da! Can I go out on the bike now! Did you get the L-plates?'

'Yes; on you go, don't forget to polish her up, and, keep off the main road!'

Hastily, I tied the plates on front and back, put on my jacket and cap and started her up.

I went down the back entry and onto the road in front of the house. I fairly whizzed up the hill and headed off towards the back-roads to practice. I wasn't long in getting the hang of it.

The engine de-coke had helped her, she would get up to 35 miles per hour with a full throttle. I loved the feeling of freedom riding along the road; made even more enjoyable by the narrow road bordered by hedges each side, giving an impression of great speed!

All too soon it was time to head for home, and I made it without any mishap. I wheeled the bike down the back path and took the L-plates off, just as Da came out of the yard.

'I will give her a good polishing and take the rust off the wheel rims.' I told him as he stood beside me. 'The silencer is blowing a wee bit so I will tighten this up before you go off to Granny's. Will you tell Uncle Jimmy, I will be all right for next Saturday again if he needs me? I am going out with the gun late on, but will give the football a miss. I really enjoyed yesterday, and I made a few bob as well.'

'I will that, but have you gone off the football?' He asked.

'No, but I will probably be leaving the BBs next year after camp, so it will give them time to try out a few more goalies. I won't miss every match.'

I got the rust of the wheel rims using the Brillo pads and polished up the wee seat and saddle bags with Ma's mansion polish. It looked like new. Da came back out with his coat and hat on and started her up.

'Sounds great William, see you when I get back. Your Ma says to tell you to go in for your dinner.'

I loved Sunday dinner, especially today's as I had shot the duck and pigeons. Ma had made a pigeon pie and roasted the duck, so I had a bit of both and they tasted great. I wondered how much the guests at the Crawfordsburn Inn were paying for theirs, with Chef Jimmy's famous orange sauce! (Sounded like Duck-la-Orangee when Jimmy said it.)

I went up to see Noel and he invited me in for a game of snooker. He had got a snooker table for his birthday and Christmas, and his birthday was Boxing Day.

I had never played snooker all that much, more billiards. Bobby Drummond, his old man, showed us a few strokes to get us started. I found it easy enough to pot the balls, but positioning the cue ball was another matter.

'I was thinking Mr Drummond, could you make a gaff for us to use when we get a dog-fish on?' (I had seen a photo of a gaff in Jean's club-book, but it was nearly six bob.)

'Give me a wee sketch of it and I will see if I can make one on the lathe,' replied Noel's Da. (He was a turner in Short and Harland's aircraft factory.)

I drew a wee sketch and put a couple of dimensions on it thinking that the old techie drawing was coming in use full, after all!

Noel's Ma made us a cup of tea and a bit of Veda bread and butter. Veda bread is like a small brown loaf, only maltier and tastier. We sat and chatted for a while and Noel suggested we went for a walk along the shore, to see if the fish were jumping. We never fished on Sundays.

We walked round by the railway station path that I took every day going to work, then over the road towards the rocks and sea. A lot of big bikes passed us as we were crossing over and one of the riders waved at me and pulled over. The rest of the bikers followed suit.

'What about you Willie?' asked one of the boys, as he removed his helmet.

'Dead on. Oh its you George, how's it going, this is my mate Noel, you know the guy who got the five shot?'

'How's it going, pleased to meet you Noel. This one (pointing at me) has been going on for weeks about your new Italian gun, a Breada is it?'

'Aye, replied Noel, 'do you shoot yourself George?'

'No, but I wouldn't mind a crack at it; I don't see much of the country living in Belfast.'

'Well, we are going out next Saturday, why not come along and I will give you a go at it. I am sure Willie will let you try his as well?'

'I fancy that right enough. Where are youse off to?'

'Round to the rocks to see if there is any fish about, we were just going for a walk. Do you want to come?'

'Sure thing, I'll just tell my mates and join you in a minute.'

George parked up his bike on the stand, locked a chain round the front wheel and joined us, as his mates took off with a roar.

'I was doing a ton tonight, along the by-pass,' said George said, quite matter of factly.

'What? a hundred miles an hour? What's it like? Can you see where you are going at that speed.' I gasped, all in the one breath.

'Well, it feels real good; you can see where you are going all right, but your eyes water if you don't wear your goggles. Don't like hitting the bees mind you, they feel like a sledgehammer at that speed,' he laughed. 'I'll take you on the back some time; both of youse, not at the same time like! And you can see for yourselves.'

We walked on in silence for a few minutes. It was a cracker of a night and soon we were scrambling across the rocks.

'This is where we fish from George,' I shouted, nearly going on my ear on wet seaweed.

'Catch much Willie?'

'Aye, Noel and I got a right few a couple of nights ago.'

Have you ever fished?'

'Yes,' replied George, 'but only on fresh water, never in the sea.' I caught a trout once, on the river Lagan.

'Well there you are then,' said Noel, 'you can come fishing as well some time – if you like.'

'And you can stay at my house, so we can get an early start. My brother is away to sea with Bibby Line,' I added.

'Sounds good to me, but what about your Ma Willie, will she mind?' asked George.

'Not at all, sure she never sees me at the weekend; I am always away early and back late. What do you think, Noel?' I asked.

'Dead on, we should be getting back before dark and the tide's coming in fast. Come on, last of the rocks is a big sissy!'

We walked slowly back towards where George had left his bike and talked about bikes and the yard. 'I just remembered! I got my licence and was out on my old mans bike today George, it was great.'

'Good Willie, get lots of practice and go for your test as soon as you can. You do yours in Ards don't you?' (Newtownards was our local driving test centre.)

'Yes,' I replied, 'I will apply in a few weeks, I can ride the bike no bother,' I boasted.

'If you pass your test I might give you a shot on the Goldie,' said George.

'You are on!' I will make sure I pass, but will have to read up on the Highway Code as some of the questions they asked my brother, when he did his bike test were hard.'

We came to George's bike and he took off the lock and chain and put on his helmet.

'Thanks boys, I enjoyed that crack; youse are so lucky to live near the sea, I will see you in work tomorrow, Willie, see you Noel,' he shouted over the roar of the gold star's exhaust, and took off waving to us.

'He's dead on Willie,' said Noel.

'I know, his bike is a buet isn't it?'

'Sure is,' replied Noel, 'but I still fancy a car, or an old van to go shooting in. We could go down to Strangford Lough shooting then, where I hear there are geese to be had, and Sean said I was ready to apply for my car test.'

'Well I'll stick to the bikes, mind you, if I got a dog, the bike wouldn't be much use unless I tied him on the back! Nah – no car for me, I'll do without a dog.'

We walked back along the railway path that I walked to and from the train every morning and night, heading towards home, talking about shooting and fishing but finishing up as usual talking about bikes; well, me anyhow.

'You know I was doing 35 miles an hour today on my Da's old bike, and I thought I was flying; imagine doing a hundred! Must be wonderful.'

'I suppose so, if you like that sort of thing and I know you do, but there is more to life than motorbikes!'

'Like what!' I replied indignantly.

'Well, you know, football, shooting, going to the flicks, birds and that,' replied Noel.

'Not for me old son! There is nothing like sitting on a bike; a sense of freedom and enjoyment, at peace with the world,' I said wistfully.

'Away you go Willie, your are a right nutcase, see you during the week,' said Noel, as we reached his gate.

'Not for me old son,' I repeated to myself, someday I will have a bike like the one George has.

I got into the house, it was very quiet and looked like everyone had turned in, except of course for Mags.

'Hope you weren't waiting up for me Mags?' I asked, sitting down to a cup of tea she had poured out for me.

'No, I was just making the pieces for tomorrow, quite a bit of that duck left over so you have a good bit of that in your piece.'

'I saw George tonight, you know, my mate from Belfast?' I asked him to stay over for a few nights some weekend, if it's okay with Ma.'

'I am sure Ma won't mind, but remember, Robert is due home next month sometime, there would be no room for George when Robert is home.'

'I am off to bed, night, night Mags,' I said as I headed up to my room. The boys were still out, so I got undressed and turned in, thinking of doing 'the ton' and the feel of a big twin throbbing between my knees!

Chapter 8

BB CAMP – THE GLASGOW STEAMER

Summer came at last and I had been in the training centre for almost a year, how the last few months had flown I was really confident at work now. I knew I had made the right decision to serve my time here at Harland's. I was eagerly looking forward to going out to my first 'outside area'.

I was told this was to be the engine works, and I would be moving to there after the summer holidays. We had a good laugh with our instructor before we went and bought him 100 Gallagher Blues, as a passing out present. He told us we could call him Alec now, wishing us all the best. He called me to the side and told me to remember to double check before cutting or machining any work. I guess he was referring to my balls-up with the Moore and Wright Engineer's Square!

Alec had let us away early after trooping us round and showing our different work places that we would go to after the summer hols. I caught the train arriving in the house with plenty of time to spare; before I had to meet the rest of the BB's lads who were going to camp. I packed a small suitcase and polished up my bugle and set off for the train station, once again.

I met the rest of the squad, and we boarded the Belfast train, pushing each other and laughing excitedly.

'Sit over here Willie,' shouted Ronnie, you can show me all the factories on the way to Belfast. Ronnie was a good mate, and worked as a painter in a local company. He didn't get out much!

'I have just got off this train about five hours ago, you know,' I answered. 'I will probably fall asleep, till we get to Belfast.'

The train made good time. We walked from Belfast station, over the Queen's Bridge, down to where the Cross-Channel Steamers berthed, and where at last we boarded the cross channel boat. She was the *Irish Coast*, and had been built at Harland's; along with her sister ship *Scottish Coast*. We were on the next leg of our journey to our annual camp. This year it was Aberfoyle in the Trossachs over the sea in Scotland.

The boat was packed, as we went down below to the sleeping berths. There were bunks in two tiers, and stretched into the gloomy distance. The lighting was very bad, I could hardly see the next person in front of me; however I was too excited to worry about that.

'Coming up top Ronnie?' I asked. We had stowed our cases underneath the bottom of the two bunks that the BB officer had told us were ours. 'We will be casting off soon, and I want to see the ships tied up at the shipyard.' (I had been told that this ship steamed right down the harbour, and also passed all the slips on which Harland's ships were being built.)

'Aye, all right Willie, I hope I am not sea-sick like the last time,' replied Ronnie.

'You will be fine, the last time we went on the Liverpool steamer, and my Da says that the Glasgow boat doesn't steam so far south, into the Irish Sea. He should know, he sailed in the Irish Sea for long enough!'

'I am sure you are right, come on, let's get a good spot on deck, to wave cheerio to old Ireland!'

We eventually made it back on deck. It seemed to take ages as we were going against passengers who coming down to the sleeping quarters. Once on deck we stood at the stern and looked over into the murky waters of the harbour. We nearly fell overboard when the ship's horn blared, the spent steam whipping away from the funnel by the wind.

'We are nearly away,' I cried. 'Look! The gangplank is being lifted in and there are men standing at the ropes ready to let go!'

'Where did you learn all this about boats Willie?' asked Davie, the officer who had joined us at the ship's rail.

'Oh I just picked it up from my Da and Uncle Jimmy; I go out fishing with him in his boat.'

Soon we were drifting away from the quay, and I heard the bells signalling the engine to start, and then the engines firing up, making the deck vibrate and as the propellers thrashed the water under the stern, the disturbed water becoming even murkier as we picked up speed and drew away from the berth. It was 9pm, so we had set sail dead on time; we were due in the Clyde at 5am. I would set my alarm and be up on deck by then, and get my first glimpse of Scotland.

We passed a lot of ships tied up at the cargo berths, they were all quiet at this time of night, but I could imagine the hustle and bustle of these when the dockers started at 7am. Robert had told me that sometimes the dockers use the dock cranes to unload the cargo, but other times they used the ships winches and cargo booms, if there were no cranes. Soon we were passing the Harland and Wolff Shipyard, and a huge notice displaying this in large letters; it also gave the current tonnage of vessels built to date.

'That's where I work, Davie, can you see that big crane? The training centre is just behind that!' I shouted excitedly.

'Aye Willie, it looks a big place, how many are there in the school?' he asked.

'Oh about a hundred apprentices all with different kinds of trades like fitters, machinists, electricians and shipwrights.'

We passed the slipways and I saw the Navy slips I had heard about; only Royal Navy vessels where built here. There were three frigates, side by side on the slips. My shipyard mate George had told me that you needed a special pass to work on the Admiralty Ships, as he called them. Further along was a large Shell tanker and two cargo ships, probably Bank Line vessels. Next the new oil refinery, which was still being built, came into view, and then we were out in Belfast Lough proper where we picked up speed.

'There's Hollywood, and over this side Carrickfergus. Look Ronnie, we will be passing close to White Head, see the lighthouse flashing?' I asked excitedly.

'Sure can, it's getting rough now, can we go back down to the bunks? I am starving and I have a big bag of tomato and cheese sandwiches that my Ma made for me,' asked Ronnie.

'No I am staying up for a while; this isn't rough. There is only a bit of a swell.'

We had started to roll a bit as well, but I enjoyed this movement, and swung easily with it. Ronnie went below; I stayed up and saw Donaghdee and the Copeland Islands lighthouses, flashing their warnings to seafarers.

On 31st January 1953 the *Princess Victoria* (the Larne to Stranraer car/passenger steamer) went down in a storm. She sank in sight of the coast, with a great loss of lives. My Da was called out, that stormy Saturday with the coastguards who assembled at Orlock Point. This was the coastguard station between Groomsport and Donaghadee; his job was to make sure that they had all their equipment ready, in case a breeches buoy was needed.

The Donaghadee and Portpatrick Lifeboats had been launched, both making it to the scene of the disaster, just off the Copeland Islands, to pick up survivors.

Another local lifeboat from Cloughey was also out in the raging seas searching for survivors.

The weather that day had been really bad, high winds, bitterly cold with hail and sleet. I remember the day vaguely; all the houses in our street had slates lifted off the roofs, and we had no electricity as the power lines had been blown down. The main cause of the ship sinking was the stern car deck doors opening and being breached in the storm. This let the sea into the car deck, the cargo shifted and these combined to cause the Princess to capsize and founder.

Over one hundred people were drowned, including nearly all the crew most of whom were from the Ports of Larne and Stranraer. There were pictures in the local paper, showing the Donaghadee Lifeboat, the *Sir Samuel Kelly*, putting survivors off at the Harbour. The coxswain, Hugh Nelson, and his crew were awarded medals and praised for being very courageous. They did not hesitate to answer the first distress call, but also after putting survivors ashore went back out again twice, making three rescue attempts in sixteen hours! The British warship, HMS *Contest*, also picked survivors from the sea, putting them ashore in Belfast. One of their POs tied a rope around his waist and jumped into the tempest rescuing a man near to drowning.

'Time you were getting below, young Scott.' I came back to present day and looked round to see the BB captain, Mr Brown standing beside me. I never noticed him I was so engrossed in the old memories and under the spell of the sea.

'Yes Mr Brown, I'll come right down. I am beside Ronnie tonight and he was saying he hoped he was not going to be sick,' I answered.

'As long as he doesn't eat too much, he should be okay.'

Oh, Oh I thought, tomato and cheese sandwiches, maybe I will be in time to stop him.

I got below, and found my bunk eventually as it wasn't any brighter, and we were told that the dimmed 'night lights' would come on at 11'o'clock, so it would become even darker soon.

'Are you up there Ronnie?' I asked, looking up to the top bunk.

'Aye Willie, but I don't feel well at all, is it awfully stormy outside, I can hear the waves against the side of the ship?'

I assured him all was well on deck, and there was a bit of a swell, but we would be turning in soon, and hopefully sleep till morning.

'Come on up to the next deck level and I will stand you a cup of tea, I noticed a lot of the boys are in the cafeteria on my way down here.' I said.

'All right Willie, if you think it will help, I need to go and pee anyhow,' answered Ronnie.

We went up to the cafeteria deck, Ronnie nipping into the bogs, on the way.

'What about you Willie, want a slug of beer?' asked one of the lads.

'No thanks, my Da says beer and ships don't mix, I would probably throw up anyhow, I don't like the stuff!' (I think my Da lost a crew member over the side, when they were fishing, and drink was involved. I had never seen my Da touch the stuff!)

'Suit yourself,' he replied and carried on passing the bottle of Guinness round a group of four or five boys. I saw him opening another, looking over his shoulder to make sure there were no BB officers around. They didn't go a bundle on booze of any kind! I was looking round for Ronnie, as he had been gone for about ten minutes. I thought he had changed his mind, and had just decided to go and look for him when he appeared round the corner.

'Over here Ronnie, I got you a good strong mug of tea with plenty of sugar in it. Are you feeling any better?' I asked hopefully, but he looked a very green round the gills.

'Never, ever, again will I eat tomato sandwiches. I just threw up in the bogs. The tomatoes floated on the top of the water, yuck! Someone had been boaked all over the floor, and I slipped on it, nearly breaking my neck when the ship rolled.' he answered vehemently.

However he took his tea and I talked to him about bikes and football and in fact anything, to keep his mind of the ship's motion, which by this time really was getting worse. The bows would lift, and then she would roll then come back down again with a clap like thunder, shuddering all the while. I noticed one or two of the boys who had been drinking, turning several shades of green (reminding me of "the forty shades of green") before rushing towards the bogs with their hands covering their mouths.

'There goes the "big hard men" hardly old enough to buy booze let alone drink it, throwing it all back down the pan.' Too late! Ronnie took off after them, bouncing off the alley-ways as the ship rolled. I finished my tea and returned our mugs to the steward at the tea counter.

'We are in for a tossing tonight, young 'un, but you seem to be coping all right.'

'Aye, so far so good, I am away to get my head down. What time do you open up again?' I asked him.

'About 4 am,' he replied. I get set up for breakfast although I don't think I will

59

sell many Ulster Fries tomorrow morning, unless it settles down during the night.'

'I will see you then, I want to be up to see us coming up the Clyde, can you see the shipyards from the boat?'

'Aye sure enough, there is a Harland's over there as well you know?' he said.

'That will be worth seeing; I work at the Belfast Shipyard, I am away to get my head down. Goodnight to you.'

I opened the bog door, only to find I had to fight my way in. The place was crowded with folk spewing up! Lo and behold, there was one of our drinkers, head nearly down the pan.

'Shift over Billy, I need a pee. Look at the state of your trousers, they are covered in boke!'

'Bugger you Scotty!' he replied, 'come to gloat?' He said, standing up.

'Just want a leak man, won't be a minute.'

I left him hanging onto a grab-rail over the bog seat, throwing up and made my way slowly down to our bunks. It was nearly dark down here and after I found our bunks, started getting undressed. I gave it up as a bad job as I couldn't keep my balance, and was starting to feel a mite queasy myself, as it was hot and stuffy down here, and didn't smell to clever either! I timed my leap into the bottom bunk, landing on top of Ronnie!

'Oach, you header!'

'Hey Ron! I thought you wanted the top bunk, you gave me a right scare there?' I whispered, as all around us boys were sleeping.

'Would you take the top one Willie?' he asked, 'I can't stay in that dammed bunk. I nearly fell out twice.'

'Well, I am certainly not sleeping beside you Ronnie you eejit! You smell awful!' I replied; and carefully climbed the small ladder up to the top bunk, hanging on for dear life when the ship rolled.

He was right though, I nearly fell out, when she rolled over to one side, then was thrown back in again as she rolled the other way. I tucked the blanket under the mattress at the front of the bunk, rolled over and tucked it in at the back of the bunk. Thus ensconced in the bunk, I fell asleep.

My alarm went off at 4 am, and as I reached under the pillow to switch it off, I noticed the comparative silence. The boat was steady as a rock; only the throb of the engines, a bit of vibration and a few rattles betrayed the fact that I was on a boat at all. I extracted myself from the blanket, and looked down, over the side of the bunk to see if Ronnie was all right. He was sleeping peacefully, with not a stitch on him. I climbed down the ladder, threw on my jumper shoes and coat, and pulling blankets over Ronnie, headed up the stairs to the deck.

It was indeed one fine morning; I could see land very close on both sides of the ship. I went back down to the cafeteria, and the steward handed me a mug of tea.

'That is usually a tanner, but seeing as you are the only one about, you can have it for nought!' he said yawning. 'Did you get a good sleep then?'

'Thanks, not bad once I got over, I woke a few times. It was quite rough during the night.' I replied.

'Quite rough! Quite rough indeed; sure it was a force six for at times, worse I have seen on this run for a while,' he said incredibly.

I took the mug of tea with the 'Burns and Laird' crossed flags on the side of it, up to the deck, and sat down on a bench-seat facing the land. A few gulls were following in our wake, which was straight as a die. They dived and scrambled for the floating bucket of galley trash that had been thrown over the stern by the cook. He was dressed in a white jacket and chequered trousers and stood smoking for a while, with his foot on the centre stern rail, watching the gulls squabbling and dipping for their breakfast and he waved up at me as he headed back to his galley.

I looked up to the hills; they were light green in the early morning light, turning to purple farther up and their tops fringed with pine trees. I found out later that the purple 'hue' was heather, very plentiful in Scottish hillsides.

Soon the other boys, all jostling with each other and yawning, joined me on the deck.

'Do we get anything to eat?' asked one of the boys.

'Not yet,' replied Davie, the officer. 'We board the coach first, and then stop at a café on the road to Stirling.'

The boat slowed down as we turned round a bend in the river Clyde. There before us were the shipyards; Harland's, then farther on some more yards Scott's was one of them, Stephen's, Fairfield's, Lithgow's, then John Brown's. They were spread out over at least a miles along the rivers banks.

'Aye Laddie, that there is the "Golden Mile" you're seeing,' said an old man, standing beside me, as the steamer slowly passed the early morning silent yards. The slips were much like ours, as were the docks; probably the same worldwide, from what I had gathered from my brother Robert.

We came astern and almost stopped as we slid alongside our berth. We were in Glasgow dockland; boy was it massive.

'Come on Bangor Boy's Brigade,' shouted Pa Brown and we all gathered up our suitcases and followed the crowd going down the gangplank.

'That was some crossing Willie,' said Ronnie, 'I was sick as a dog all night, and you snoring like a pig above me didn't help matters'

'Well I enjoyed it, especially coming up the Clyde; I will never forget the sun on the hills, and the tall pine trees, so peaceful and tranquil in the morning light.'

'Hark at him,' jeered Billy. 'Poet in the making!'

'You are looking a bit better now than the last time I saw you,' I replied grinning. 'You were wearing a bog seat round your neck then and calling for Hughieee…'

We boarded the coach and I took a last look back at the steamer, she was a fine ship, I thought, bringing us safely across such a rough sea. Little did I know, but I was to cross this sea many, many times, both as passenger and ships engineer, in the years to come.

Chapter 9

ON SCOTTISH SOIL

The coach moved slowly towards the dock gate, where a policeman waved us through, seemed strange to see a cop without a gun strapped to his waist. Soon we were on a big road, with two lanes.

'This is the biggest road I have ever seen, what's it called Mr Brown?' Asked Ronnie, now fully recovered and looking forward to his breakfast.

'This is a motorway, and we are on the dual carriageway part. There are bigger ones than this in England, he explained, 'some have three lanes.'

We passed the rock of Dumbarton, and pulled into a café, with everyone cheering and shouting.

'Keep it down boys, we don't want to upset the natives,' one of the officers quipped.

We all piled off the bus and headed into the café. Practically everyone had bacon, eggs and fried bread, these Scottish people had never heard of potato bread, or soda bread. (In Ireland these were part of a fry-up.) However, they put a black pudding on our plates, but we all gave this a wide berth, when they told us what it was made from – pigs blood!

We had a quick shuftie in the souvenir in the shop next door to the café, then all climbed back aboard the bus, for the final part of our journey to Aberfoyle. We sang as we sped along the road, the old bus slowing down a bit as we hit the country roads, which were not unlike the roads at home. There were mountains everywhere; at home we only had Black Mountain above Belfast, and, of course the Mountains of Mourne at Newcastle.

There were also a lot of loughs, rivers and farmland; again the farms and animals were very much like the ones in County Down, but having more sheep than us. We passed small villages, and the people waved back to us as we cheered and waved to them.

'This is some country Willie, look at those mountains, you can't see the tops for the clouds, must be miles high.' said Ronnie

'Sure thing, I think we are going to like Scotland, my Da was saying they talk funny, but are good crack!' I replied, craning my neck sideways to the window to see the peaks.

We reached the village of Aberfoyle, and were soon climbing up a winding track towards a distant forest. The camp appeared round a bend and the cheering and shouting reached a crescendo as we pulled up at a long, low log cabin.

'Everybody out,' bawled one of the officers. 'Let the ladies out first boys, show a bit of manners!'

The ladies were the officer's wives. Four officer's wives had come along with us, and up to now we had not seen much of them. We knew them all of course, as they had made our costumes for the panto last year, and applied copious amounts of make-up to us budding stars of the future. (I don't think!)

We were told to line up in the wooden cabin. It was very large inside and had tables and chairs and what looked like a counter. It was in fact the 'canteen' where we would have our meals and morning and evening prayers

'Right boys, this is the cookhouse, and these lovely ladies will be cooking our meals, but we will have to help them prepare the food, (peel the spuds he meant! I had been to camp before) and clean up the kitchen. Still we are here for a fort-night, so we should be able to share these fatigues out and still have plenty of fun.'

He called out the team leaders and then the teams, which would share the tents. These were large 'bell tents' which held about eight boys. We all took off to our allotted tents and started to unpack the essentials. The rest of our gear we kept in the suitcases, beside our camp beds. These were not beds as such, a few blankets and thin mattresses, which we could roll up during the day to give us a bit more room. The ground sheet was spotless and our team leader, an NCO told us we had to keep it clean for morning inspections.

'And, don't, touch the sides or top of the tent when it is raining or…'

'We know! It will leak and we will all get soaked,' we pre-empted him.

'Once you are settled in go out for a walk, not too far mind you to get your bearings. Remember, it will soon be teatime. 'Willie! Don't go too far, we are on bugle duty today and tomorrow, so you will have to sound the calls.'

The calls were part of camp routine and I enjoyed this, as it was like we were in the army barracks. It started at 8am with Reveille, and the hoisting of the flag, and then 1st and 2nd meal calls throughout the day and ended with Last Post, the lowering of the flag and finally Lights Out. It was a bit daunting that first morning call as all was quiet, and if you made a mistake, everyone knew about it and slagged you off.

I blew the dinner calls "Come to the cook-house door boys!" and headed down to the cookhouse. The tea was great, the ladies had done a superb job, I had got out of 'fatigues' as I was on bugle duty, but had to help wash up afterwards. We were all full after tea, and Ronnie, Jim (another good mate) and I strolled down the lane into the village. It was very quiet, for a Friday night. All the shops were closed, but we found a wee souvenir shop, and we wandered in there.

'Hello boys, are you the yins camped up on yon hill?' asked the man in the shop, in a strange tongue.

'Yes,' we chorused together. 'It sure is quiet around here, not that we are complaining,' I added hastily.

'Weel now, you ken it's nearly eight of the clock, the shops shut at seven, except Friday, when they stay open later, and, o' course we dinna open on the Sabbath!'

We bought a few postcards, said goodnight to the man and wandered on down the street.

'Look!' shouted Jimmy, pointing at a notice pinned to a telegraph pole. 'There's a fair coming on Monday. Just what we needed, that should live things up a bit!'

We walked on to the end of the street, and came to a wee park of sorts, with a path leading to a footbridge over a river.

'Lets have a look in the river guys!' I shouted. We ran across to the bridge, stopping in the middle to look into the clear water.

'Sure is deep', said Ronnie loudly.

'Shush!' I replied quietly, 'see the fish down there, beside the big stones?'

'Where? Oh yes, there is three or four of them, wonder what they are?'

'They's troot, and you need a licence to fish here, you ken!'

I nearly fell into the water, looking round I saw a very big man in a kilt! Crooked over one arm, with the breech open, hung a shotgun. It looked like a toy in his arm. A black and white border collie sat at his heel.

'I am the gillie roun here and work for the squire, you are welcome to walk along the river, but ney fishing withoot a permit. ye ken'

'I like your gun,' I said. 'Do you get much to shoot over here?'

'You'll be Irish, I am thinking, are you at the camp on the hill?' he answered. 'And aye, we do no bad, (we waited, and sure enough, he finished) you ken.'

'Yes, we are from Northern Ireland, from a wee town just outside Belfast. We are here for a fortnight. I have a shotgun at home; a single barrel.' I finished excitedly.

'I only caught half of that, you don't half talk funny, mun!'

'Well, I shoot at home, going after the wood pigeon and duck,' I said slowly.

'That's guid man, we must have a yarn sometime afore you gang hame!' he said walking away towards the riverbank.

'What did he say Willie about a gang?' asked Jimmy.

'Dinna ken,' I laughed. 'Come on, hurry up you two, time we were getting back, I have to play the last post!'

We walked back to camp, still trying to decipher between us what kiltie man had said, and wondering what a gillie was. I was quite chuffed that he had called be a man, albeit a mun!

We had supper of drinking chocolate and big pieces of bread and jam, as much as we wanted. I was helping with the clearing up, when our NCO came in and told me to blow Last Post as everyone was waiting to go to bed!

I stood beside the flag, and as I finished the last note I had the wonderful experience of hearing the last few bars echo across the mountains above us and down into the glens beneath. It was a quiet, peaceful night, hardly dark at all, even at ten thirty. The vision stayed with me as I pulled the blanket over me.

'Psst, Willie!' I came awake to Ronnie shaking me. 'Come on we are going out blackening the new boys tonight. The NCO is over in the hall with the rest of the officers; now's our chance!'

The blackening up of the first timers was a ritual. We old timers would sneak into the new boy' tents and put black boot polish on their goolies. I suppose it was pitiless, but we all had to go through it. (I remember my first camp, wakening up and going for a pee and finding my privates covered in boot polish. It stung like blazes) I got the boot polish and followed Ronnie and Jimmy out of our tent.

'In here, this is the one we are doing,' whispered Jimmy.

Our dastardly deed done we headed back to our tent, just in time to see the hall door opening, spilling light onto the nearest tents.

'Made it just in time, here comes Albert the NCO.'

'Don't think I didn't see youse three creeping about out there,' he said.

'Just let it be the last time after lights out, unless you need a pee.'

'Dead on Albert, but Jimmy was a bit sick and I went with him to the bogs,' I lied.

'Do you think I came up the Lagan on a bubble, Willie? I know what youse were up to so get turned in! I will call you for Reveille.'

I got back under the blankets and cleaned my hands on a piece of cloth. There was not much blackening on them, but I didn't want to get caught out in the morning.

On Sunday morning the band formed up with two NCOs carrying the colours leading us in the band. We were followed by the rest of the company as we marched smartly down the lane to church parade.

'Band, Band! – Homeward, Faraway and Forest – (this was one of our favourite marches) on my whistle,' shouted our bandmaster Billy Gordon. He was a well-liked and much respected officer, who also took us for PT.

The side-drummers started up, along with Nicky on the base with his newly acquired leopard skin tied around his middle. We got this as well as the cup for winning the band contest. We buglers followed after their first couple of introductory drum rolls, the sound echoing over the mountains and glens. There was quite a crowd of people watching us from the pavement as we marched through the town to the Church of Scotland Kirk, with our colours blowing in the slight breeze.

Billy blew his whistle, and we finished up the march, wheeling smartly into the churchyard.

We fell out and settled into the church. I nearly burst out laughing at all the first timers scratching their nether regions, due I suspected to out nocturnal jaunts around the tents, with our Cherry Blossom boot polish.

After church service, we formed up outside again, and marched back to camp, playing our hearts out. Butter wouldn't melt in their mouths. (I don't think!)

I noticed a lot of the men wore kilts, and short jackets looking very smart. One of men waved over to me; it was the kiltie (Ye Ken) from last night at the river. I nodded back as we marched on up the lane back to camp.

Chapter 10

GILLIES, TROUT, AND A PADDLE STEAMER

Ronnie and I went for a walk after dinner. Jimmy was turning in for a snooze, but said he would maybe catch up with us later. We walked for a few miles through the forest and came to another stream, probably part of the same river we saw last night. I had a piece of string and a bent pin with me, just in case!

I turned over a stone and gathering up a couple of red earthworms sat on the bank, watching the river.

'Come sit down here Ronnie, and be quiet!' I whispered. I tied the safety pin to the string and then the string to a piece of a stick, I had been carrying. I lay down flat on my tummy and putting the worm on the end of the pin, dropped it into the river, close to the bank. The current carried it into the middle of the river. I sneaked back up the bank and sat down to watch the end of the stick.

We didn't have to wait long, the end of the stick gave a twitch, and I pulled it back over my head. Up came string, complete with a small fish on the end and flew over my head to land in the grass behind me. The wee fish had unhooked itself and lay thrashing about gasping in the grass. I wet my hands in the river and picked it up and carefully put it back into the stream, holding it in my hand under the water to let it get its bearings.

'See the way it swam away Ronnie? If you aren't careful with fish, you can damage them, and they die.' I whispered.

'Is that right now mun?' This cudney be the same mannie I spoke to but yesterday aboot needing a permit to fish and, on the Sabbath as well, shame on you! and with you just new by coming from the Kirk?' What's your name Mun?' asked the gillie.

'It's Willie, and this is Ronnie, but he had nothing to do with this. It was all my idea. He is not really with me!' I wailed.

'Hold your weist, laddie. Have I no been watching yew frae behind yon bush for the past half oor or more? Do you no ken you are on the Laird's land? Still I saw the way you handled the wee brownie, so no herm done eh, ye ken?'

'Thanks very much mister, I saw you at church this morning, you looked very smart in your kilt,' I answered gratefully.

'No need for your airs and graces, me name's Rory, and dinna try tae soft-soap me, laddie. If you like I will take you beath fushing sometime, for real fish, na small yins like that brownie,' he said

'Would you Rory? What's a brownie?'

'Broon troot, laddie, the river is fair full of them, but further on there are bigger yins. I usually catch a few for the Laird's supper, and my own too, if he but kent!'

We arranged to meet on Tuesday at two o'clock at the footbridge on the outskirts of town, telling us to 'keep this tae yersells' as the Laird might get to hear about it – ye ken!

Ronnie didn't want to come, so I met Rory as planned at the bridge. He carried two long cane rods, with thick fishing line attached to a centre pin reels, and a telescopic rod with a net on the end of another rod, and of course he had the dog at his feet.

'Meet Bracken Wullie,' he said as I came up to him.

'Hi Bracken, aren't you are just lovely? I bet he is a good retriever,' I said as we started walking down the riverbank.

'Aye, and he rounds up the yows as weel. We hae aboot forty of they,' he said.

'What's yows?' I asked.

'Thought you hailed from the country, laddie?' Yows is sheep! D' yew no ken?'

'Oh, I see, look! I saw a rise over that side of the bank,' can we have a go at her?'

'Aye, tak yer time laddie, and whist, you are bawling like a bullock!'

Rory showed me how to tie on a fly to the leader and cast over the water, by swinging my arm back and forwards over my shoulder, whilst letting out more line. The thick line floated on the water, but the thin nylon trace line and fly sank, moving swiftly downstream with the river current.

'This is great, Rory, what do you call this sort of fishing?' I whispered.

'This is fly fushin, laddie, and the king of sports. No for me yon worms of yers. This is the only way to fish!' he enthused, in that lovely, lilting voice.

No sooner had he said that, than he let out a whoop, like a war cry scaring me to half to death, and nearly causing me to drop the rod. Bracken barked excitedly, looking up at his master, his tail wagging in circles.

'Got yin Wullie! Whist dug, gae me a bit o room tae land it, grab yon net and get ready to catch it as it comes doon the side o' the bank.' Boy was he excited!

'I have it! Rory!' I have it I shouted as the trout swam into the net. This was a much better idea than gaffing the fish I thought, I will see big Noel's Da about making one when we get home again.

That was the only fish we caught, but it was a beauty and will stay in my memory forever; wait till I tell Da I thought. It was brown speckled, slim and long, and what a fight it had put up. I was hooked! I had to try this at home!

'I am off to the market for t' week with the Laird Wullie, but na doot we will have another shot at the brownies afore you gaun back o'er the sea. I'll wait at the yon bridge again next Friday nict about seven, if you want to tae gang for a stroll. Ye ken.' We both chorused as we parted.

'I look forward to that Rory, I really do. I enjoyed myself today, and I am starting to understand your lingo,' I replied walking towards the village.

'Off with ye mun, yours is near as bad, but better than a Sassenach!' (whatever that was) he shouted over his shoulder as he turned and walked away, his kilt swinging in time with that peculiar gait of his.

'Hey Willie! Over here!'

This shout was from Ronnie and Jimmy, standing beside a man dressed like a gypsy. I walked over to them.

'This is Hamish, Willie; he owns the fairground. We were just chatting before going over there. Are you coming?' he asked.

They were standing beside a small man, in shirtsleeves, a broad leather belt holding up greasy brown corduroy trousers. He wore a red checked a neckerchief and was a decidedly scruffy and suspect looking bit of goods.

'Sure thing!' I replied. 'What about you Hamish?'

'And whit sort of tongue is that,' he greeted me.

'Och, not you as well! Can you not understand the Queen's English?'

He never replied, just cleared his throat and spat at the ground as we set off along the river and soon came to the fairground, which had Buddy Holly's 'Rave-On' blasting out. There were the usual kiddie's rides, dodgems and the waltzers. The sideshows looked good crack and I headed for the rifle stall.

I gave a tanner to the gypsy women behind the stall, who was wearing what must have been the world's largest gold (or brass) hooped earrings. She handed me six lead slugs and a Diana air rifle, which was chained to the counter.

'Not a very trusting lot, are you?' I joked, as I broke the air rifle and inserted a slug. She shook her head and never answered, just pointed towards the targets.

I managed to get four bulls and won a Scottish kiltie doll. That would do for Mags, as she liked ornamental dolls. I asked for another go, but she refused me saying it was time to close. A likely story I thought!

We returned to camp and, after supper, the captain told us we were going across Loch Lomond on a paddle steamer the next day. Only thing was we had to set off at six tomorrow morning for a place called Balloch (pronounced Bal-loch). This caused a lot of guffaws from the boys, and a few raised eyebrows from the officer's wives.

We boarded the *Maid of the Loch* bright and early the next morning. She was tied up alongside the wooden pier at Balloch and sure enough was a genuine paddle steamer – the real McCoy!

I looked down to the engine room, the smell of steam and hot oil wafting up to me. The big open crankcase with the cranks and long shining levers began turning slowly, as we moved off the pier. Wouldn't mind a shuftie at that I thought, but there was a large notice posted at the engine room door, prohibiting entry by passengers.

She must have been a coal or wood burner, I thought as she belched clouds of smoke from her stack as she picked up speed. However she was remarkably steady, with little vibration coming from her wee steam engine and once we were underway, the smoke eased to a trickle, with a whisper of steam through it.

It was a glorious day and we passed numerous small islands. Some of them had one or two wee houses on them, with shingle paths leading down to wooden jetties at the shore. There were a few with a skiffs tied up alongside the jetties. Some islands looked uninhabited and I imagined what it would be like camping out there, fishing from the shores, and cooking the fish over a campfire – my mouth watering at the thought!

One of the deckhands standing beside us pointed to a very smart motorboat; its brasses and varnished wood shining as it veered off towards one of the islands small landing piers.

'That will be the mails boys, she carries the letters, parcels and provisions from Balloch to all the islands,' he said rather wistfully. He told us later that he was an Islander from Barra, (wherever that was!) and missed the island way of life.

We had a great day, with sandwiches and lashings of good strong tea aboard and all to soon it was time to turn round and head back to Balloch. We disembarked down the rickety gangway and onto the wooden pier.

'Are you for the Fair tonight Willie?' asked Ronnie. 'Jimmy and I are going to try the waltzers. Did you see the dolly-birds there last night? They were all round the waltzers and dodgems.'

'Naw, I will give them and the birds a miss, though I may get my fortune told by the Gypsy Rose Lee look-alike,' I replied. 'Remind me after lights out tonight and I will tell you a story about a gypsy woman.'

Chapter11

SUPERSTITION, SPORTS DAY AND CASTLES WITH GHOSTIES

We were all turned in later that night and Jimmy asked me if I had had my fortune told.

'Yes,' I replied. 'I am going to travel the world and move over to Scotland to live, according to old Rosie Lee.'

Laughs of derision followed from all corners of the bell-tent, followed by a few pillows.

'You don't believe all that malarkey Willie, do you?' asked Albert.

'Course I do let me tell you a story, my Da told us at home.' I said, and started re-telling his story.

One time, when my Da worked his family's fishing boat, they had fallen on hard times. There were no herring to be had, and they had pulled their boat up on the shore to caulk and pitch her bottom.

Granny Scott was on her own in the house, when a gypsy-woman knocked on the door asking if she wanted to buy any ribbons or clothes pegs. Granny told her she had no money, but asked her in for a cup of tea and a piece of jam and bread. The old gypsy was starving, and nearly ate her out of house and home, but she told Granny her fortune, to pay for her tea.

'Before this week's out the top of this table we are sitting at will be covered with silver.' She said, in her foreign sounding brogue. 'Mark you my words missus, this is very true, I wouldn't lie to you as you have been very kind to me.'

Well, she went off and soon the men folk were back in for their tea, and Granny told them about the gypsy. Now the fishermen are very, very, superstitious and they believed every word, hoping that the silver on the table she foretold meant that the herring were coming back The next day they launched the boat and steamed out to the fishing grounds, but alas came back empty handed.

The next morning, my Da was down at the boat, and looking up saw a big fleet of Royal Navy warships, swinging of their anchors in the bay just off Bangor.

He ran home like mad and told Granda. He made a big notice from cardboard – 'Sail round the battleships, a shilling each.' he painted on it with big letters. They all set off for the boat and put up the notice at the pier.

Soon the boat was filling with tourists, all clambering aboard at a bob a time. They never stopped all day, sailing back and forth around the warship, as many times as they could, because they had learned that the warships were sailing on the evening tide. At the end of the day they all trooped tiredly up to the house and Granda emptied the bag of silver shillings onto the table. They had made enough money to keep them going for a few weeks, by which time the herring should be back again....

I finished to silence.

'Do youse not get it?' I asked exasperated and dry as a bone, as I had been talking uninterrupted for about fifteen minutes. I presumed they had been following the story.

'The silver shillings was the silver on the table that the gypsy woman had prophesised?' asked Ronnie, 'and not the silver herring scales?'

'The penny has dropped,' I quipped.

'Good yarn Willie,' said the NCO, now get turned in, it's sports day tomorrow!'

It was another great day. They get lovely weather over here, I thought, but I don't go a bundle on the midges! We played five-a-side football, ran the usual races, had the high and long jumps, finishing off with a picnic out on the field. At prize giving I was awarded half a dollar for having the longest goal kick! Well, I should hope so, I had taken plenty, but that was my lot.

The week wore on, the weather staying perfect throughout and I was getting a good tan as I spent most days climbing the mountains and paddling about the cold streams. These were plentiful and which down the mountains, through the forest and glens. This was truly a beautiful place to have a camp, I thought although some of the youngsters were getting restless and a bit bored.

One night after supper we were told that we would be going on a trip to Stirling Castle! After breakfast, again in the glorious summer sunshine we boarded the old bus.

Stirling was a big town, compared to Bangor anyhow, with stacks of shops. We did the souvenir shops first then visited the castle, amazed at the drawbridge, ramparts and dark, dank dungeons.

We had sandwiches and buns at the teashop before wondering off again to explore the dungeons, which had fascinated us on the guided tour.

'This is where the kings held their prisoners, and tortured them before cutting their heads off with a big sword,' whispered Jimmy. 'There are probably ghosts with no heads roaming around here, pulling chains after them at midnight!'

'Be quiet, Jimmy,' said Ronnie, 'you are giving me the creeps!'

It was certainly scary down here, in the dim light with the sound of dripping water echoing from somewhere close.

'Let's go back up,' I suggested, letting a loud yell out of me, and the boys fled up the steps in from of me like a banshee was chasing them!

We wandered back up to the battlements, where there were some fine old guns, with round black shot piled neatly beside them.

'Aye laddies, this is what we used against the Sassenachs!' said an old man in the dress of a Scottish soldier – kilt, plaid and bonnet as he leaned on his large broadsword. There was the pearl handled hilt of a wee dagger, sticking out the top of one of his tartan stockings. 'We fair gid them whit for! A few shots from this yin and they all fled.' He reminisced, patting the gun barrel fondly

I could see it all in my mind's eye; the redcoats storming the castle, their officers on horseback, with long swords drawn urging them on, with the Scottish Kilties blasting away with the cannons, and shrieking obscenities at them. They must have been a fearsome sight; bawling in their native tongue their long, wild ginger hair and beards flowing in the wind, swinging their broadswords over their heads. Enough to frighten the life out of any sane body!

We all piled back onto the coach and sang all the way to Aberfoyle. We had learnt a few Scottish ballads in the choir, and sang "Scottish Soldier" and "Will ye no come back again", as we made our way over the hills and through the Scottish glens.

Chapter 12

HASTE YE BACK

I had arranged to meet Rory at the old bridge at seven o'clock, and I was afraid I had missed him until Bracken ran up to me, barking and wagging his tail as a greeting. He was a typical collie, smooth silk-like black and white coat, panting noisily with his pink tongue hanging out the side of his smiling mouth.

'Aye laddie, see you made it then. What hiv ye bin up tae?' greeted Rory

'I was away at Stirling Castle. I got a few souvenirs to take home and I saw the castle. It is some size. I could see for miles from the battlements.'

That wis the idea, ye ken, tae see yon English in plenty of time tae warn the villagers to come into the castle tae git looked after, ye ken!'

We wondered along the bank and then Rory took me through the woods, to see the young grouse being raised, in huts not unlike our chicken coups at home. Once reared these would be set loose on the hill. He said that the English liked to shoot the full-grown grouse on the heather. The game season started on 12th August and was known as the "glorious twelfth".

'I havny the time ta go fushin today laddie, but I will take you round the oothouses of the estate,' he said. 'Stay close to me now, and dinna touch anything! Yon flag flying tells you the Laird is at hame, ye ken!' Pointing with his shepherds crook to the flag, flying from the flagpole on the big house.

He took me round the stables and sheep pens, showing me where they dipped the sheep, to keep the beasties of them! Then he showed me their Highland cattle. These were wild-eyed beasts with beautiful long silky, brown and red coats. Long curved wicked sharp horns grew from their bony, shaggy heads.

'We tak they beasts to yon Royal Show at Edinburgh, and have won a few rosettes, the Laird keeps them in the big hoose, the rosettes, ye ken!' pointing at the cattle.

Strolling on a bit more, we came to another wee wooden hut he called a bothy. We went inside and he brewed up a can of tea. We sat for a while in companionable silence, sipping our black mugs of tea.

'I will no see you afore you gang, laddie, so here's a wee present, ye ken, to mind ye of me and Bracken.'

He handed me a small wooden box, beautifully hand made, about the size of a swan matchbox.

'Dinna open it the noo, laddie, it's only a wee minder' he said, 'come on and I'll walk a bit with ye, and see ye till yon road end.'

We walked on, again in silent companionship, with me wishing that I had got him something, but knowing that I would only have embarrassed him, if I had.

'God go with you son and a safe journey hame, I hiv enjoyed yir company, so I hiv.'

'Bye Rory,' I whispered, with a croak in my throat. 'I'll never forget you and Bracken.'

We parted company at the old bridge, and he was still standing there, when I looked back, the perfect Highland gentleman, leaning on his Shepherd's crook with Bracken at his feet.

I met the boys at the fairground, which was going full swing. It was packed with folk, and there had one of the Beatles hits blasting out across the field. What a contrast I thought!

'What about you Willie, are you for a shot on the dodgems? Come and meet Kirsty and Jeannie, they are sisters.' greeted Ronnie.

'Hi girls, who's who? I asked.

'I'm Kirsty, and this is my wee sister Jeannie,' answered the older of the two. 'Are you taking us onto the dodgems?'

She had a beautiful accent, and was very pretty. I paid for Kirsty and she jumped into a dodgem car, pulling me on beside her, much to the chagrin of Ronnie, who was by this time left on his own. Jimmy had taken Jeannie onto the waltzers. I let Kirsty drive and she was pretty good – for a girl!

'How come I can understand what you are saying?' I asked her, 'everyone else over here speaks double Dutch!'

'Och, I have been at Glasgow University, so I have probably lost some of my Chuckter twang,' she answered. But not her Chuckter charm, I thought. Pity we were going home tomorrow!

I left the girls with Jimmy and Ronnie and headed up the hill to the camp. I went into our tent and opened the box that Murdo had given me. Inside was a sprig of lucky white heather and a tiny trout fly, mounted expertly on a piece of varnished wood.

'Thank you Rory,' I whispered to myself; I'll not forget you.

It was raining the next morning as we packed up our gear and made our way to the coach. The mist covered the mountains, but the air was fresh and clean, with the unforgettable smell of pine trees, heather and peaty soil.

We had an uneventful journey back to Glasgow and boarded the steamer for Belfast.

'Did you enjoy yourself Willie?' asked our NCO as we pulled away from the side of the dock.

'Dead on, I'll remember Scotland for a while. Did I tell you I can speak the lingo now?' I asked.

'Go on then!'

'It's a braw, brict, munlight nict, the nict, ye ken' I replied, to the laughs of the boys around us.

As the steamer left the quay, I looked over to the docks and onto the hills beyond. I'll be back, I vowed, yes sir, I'll be back!

Chapter 13

MY SECOND YEAR

It was Monday morning already; it felt like I had never been away. But I was cheerful enough as I was going to start work in the engine works today.

I walked into the large workshop, I had been shown where to go the day before the holidays. There were still red, white and blue streamers along the roof girders. I supposed that these had been put up for the Twelfth. I stopped, looking about for the time clock.

'What are you stood there for boy and what's your name?' asked a gaffer in a green dustcoat and black bowler.

'William Scott, I am starting here today, and was looking for the time clock,' I answered.

'Follow me boy!'

We walked, well, at least he walked and I half ran to keep up with his long strides back outside the shop and stopped outside a hut. It had a door at the side and a sliding glass window half way up the front. Greencoat rattled on the door and walked in, signalling me to follow.

'Got a new start for you Billy; just out of the training school by the look of him. Sort him out, and then send him back to my office. I will see where he is to go!' He said to Billy as he pushed passed me, shutting the door on the way out.

'Don't I know you son?' Billy asked rather kindly, 'your family goes to our church on the Clandeboye Road, don't they?'

'Yes, that's right, you're Mr Hutton aren't you?' I replied, grateful at last to see a friendly face that I knew.

'Scott, now let me see. Yes, got your board here. We don't have time clocks out here; everyone has a board like this, with their number on it. We have put your number on this one. You pick this up here every morning, and line up outside the time hut, passing it back through the window to me at night, when the horn blows. You get your pay packet here also, on Friday nights. I'm your timekeeper from now on, William.' he finished.

The wooden board was not very thick and about three inches long by an inch and a half wide. It had my old clock number branded into the oily wood.

'Thanks, Mr Hutton, I will see you at five, who was the gaffer that brought me in here?'

'Oh, that's big Eddie Schoffield. He is the head foreman of the engine works. His bark's worse than his bite, but don't mess him around.' he advised me.

I walked back inside the shop and over towards big Eddie's office. I climbed the stairs, knocked, and opening the door, walked slowly up to his desk.

'I'm back, Mr Schoffield. I got my board from the timekeeper,' I said shakily, looking round the busy office. Out of the windows I could see the whole of the engine works in front of me. What a view! I found out later that the gaffers kept an eye on everyone from up here – the office in the sky!

'Right boy, come along with me, I will introduce you to your journeyman. Do as he says and you will learn your trade well. Willie Ross is one of our best marine fitters.' said Greencoat, fairly going down the office stairs, two at a time.

That magic word; marine fitter – I was on my way at last!

We walked down a roadway on the shop floor, between two yellow lines about twelve feet apart. The floor was made of black wooden blocks, all laid neatly and tightly together. On each side of the shop stretched long rows of benches, where the men and boys were working at their vices and looking at drawings. Between the benches and the yellow passageway was a lay-down area for the different engine components. We stopped and walked over to one of the benches, picking our way carefully between the machined and forged engine-parts.

'Here we are then, Scott. Meet your journeyman, Willie Ross.'

Willie Ross was a wee man wearing a brown boiler suit, over a shirt and tie, grey wispy hair escaped from the flat cap on his head. He came over from the bench, rubbing his hands with a piece of waste and looking at me over the top of his glasses on the way across. I straightened up and shook hands with Willie.

'Pleased to meet you Mr Ross.' I said, looking round apprehensively

'Aye, likewise I'm sure. Call me Willie, by the way.' Nodding to Greencoat. 'This your first move?'

'Yes,' I replied. 'This is my first move, I have been dying to get out of the training school.'

'Well, I suppose it was a bit like prison, but that don't mean it is any easier out here, eh Willie?' said Greencoat. 'Weren't no training school in our day.'

With that he ignored me and went on to talk to Willie about the day's work, and left, giving me nod and ever so slight half wink.

'What do you like to be called?' asked Willie.

'William, usually, my second name's Scott,' I ventured.

'Well, William, let's get on with it, Big Eddie, the gaffer, don't like slackers!'

He showed me a drawing of an engine governor gear and asked if I knew what it was. I replied that it was an engine part, and I could recognise a few bits of it lying on the floor, and on the bench.

'Good lad, put that shaft on the bench, carefully now, and come with me to the stores.'

We walked up to the stores, passing below the gaffer's office. I looked up and there was big Eddie, arms folded, looking through the large dirty windowpane over his domain.

Willie introduced me to the store man, John Cowan, and ordered up a piece of key steel. John went away and returned with the steel, marked it up in his book and asked me for my board number. I rattled this off, and took the key steel.

We walked back down to our bench, Willie nodded at a few of the men, and they nodded back to him, but just stared at me. I measured and marked out the piece of tool steel, under the watchful eye of Willie, rechecking the drawing and my measurements twice.

'That's the way boy, double check everything, before you cut it,' said Willie, 'don't make too many mistakes that way. We only get as much key steel to do the job. If we need any more, big Eddie has to sign for it, and he will want to know why you need an extra bit. He's no too keen on us wasting material. All gaffers are the same; profit, profit, and more profit!' He spat.

The hooter went at half twelve, I couldn't believe the morning had gone so quickly. I was enjoying myself and Willie had a wry old sense of humour. I thought I was going to like him. I hoped so anyway. We were stuck with each other for the next six months, or so.

'Here's my tea-can, boy, away up yonder to those sinks and fill it with hot water,' instructed Willie, pointing to an area where steam was rising from a row of taps, over a stainless steel trough. All around this a queue of men and boys had formed.

I took off like a shot and I got in line. After I had filled Willie's tea-can with hot water, I carefully put the lid back on as the steam was roasting my hand, and walked back down the shop with it.

'I will make your tea, if you like Willie, I used to help my Da on the building sites. I made the men's tea over the fire.'

'No; it's all right, I like mine strong. Hey Effie, come and meet my new boy!' he called over to the man on the next bench.

'This is William; he says he can wet the tea, maybe we will try him out tomorrow Eh?'

'How are you William, settling in all right?' asked Effie, gripping my hand. He had the same grip as Willie, moving his pinkie finger over mine. (I was to find out later that this was a Mason's handshake!)

'Yes thanks Effie, can I go to the canteen now Willie?'

'Aye, all right, make sure you are not late back though, big Eddie walks along the benches as soon as the hooter goes. Most folk take their piece at the bench.'

I ran up to the canteen and sat down at our table. We stared at the new boys lining up at the counter. They looked a right gawky lot with their spotless boiler suits. Not a patch on us old hands!

'How did you all get on?' I asked to no one in particular.

'Okay,' chorused the boys, chewing on their sandwiches and slupping their tea manfully.

'I'm in the boiler shop Willie,' said Nicks, 'It is very noisy and a black hole of a place, but the crack is good.'

'I'm in the engine works fitting shop' I told everyone, 'my journey man seems dead on.'

'You're lucky,' said one of the other boys, (who was a bit full of himself), 'mine is a crabbit old git! He said I knew nothing and was there to learn and not talk so much!'

I looked at my watch; it was five to one. I stood up saying cheerio to the boys, and ran down the road to the shop.

Willie and Effie were lying on the bench, with their caps off and the newspaper over their eyes. They jumped as the horn blew and put their caps back on (I noticed Willie was quite bald) and the newspapers in their jackets, which were hung on a couple of nails in the wall.

'Back to porridge William, let's have a look at that last key you fitted to that shaft, looks a bit squint to me.'

We were examining this when big Eddie's head appeared between us.

'How's your boy getting on Willie? Will we have to send him back to the school?'

'Just checking this key, looks a good fit, but I should hope so, he took half the day to fit it!'

I took this as a compliment, and started to fit a bush to the shaft.

'Show me this on the blueprint boy!' Barked big Edd.

I jumped at least a foot, and pointed out the component I was fitting on the drawing.

'Good, know what it is?'

'Aye, Mr Schoffield, Willie told me it was part of the governor gear,' I replied confidently.

'And what does a governor do?'

'Well, I think it controls the engine speed and slows down the engine when the propeller comes up out of the water,' I replied, crossing my fingers. (Brother Robert had told me about the engine over speeding, when the prop came clear of the sea.)

'Very good!' he replied, winked at Willie and walked over to talk to Effie.

I continued to fit the shaft to the brass bush, marking the shaft with engineers blue, and scraping off the high spots, with Willie's scraper.

Big Eddie came back over and told Willie to share me with Effie, until his boy was back at work.

'Did you hear that boy? Effie's boy is in hospital and won't be back for a few weeks; crashed on one of them dammed motorbike contraptions. Death traps they are! Away up to the stores and ask for a set of half round scrapers boy, you are going to ruin my one if you carry on like that. Is that the way they showed you in the training school?'

'Yes,' I replied meekly, 'am I not doing it right?'

'Just get the store scrapers and I will show you,' he replied quietly.

I went up to the stores and got a set of scrapers from John. I had to hand him my board. He told me I would get it back when I returned the scrapers to the store, saying that this way the tools wouldn't wander!

'Right now William, use the smallest scraper, and hold it in the middle with you left hand, not so tight or you will cut yourself. Now, hold the handle in your right hand, and turn the blade slowly and lightly from right to left, scraping off the marking blue. You were being very heavy-handed with mine, and I don't want you ruining it. I will show you how to sharpen the edge with an oil stone in a minute, this store scraper looks blunt.'

I carried on myself for a while and lost concentration for a minute, gouging the brass and leaving a score mark on the bearing. Whack! Willie clipped me over the head with his cap. (One of about a million clips Willie was to give to me!)

'Concentrate boy! That bearing cost a fortune to cast and machine, you nearly ruined it!' shouted Willie.

I was mortified, and sore; more from the knowing looks of the other men and leers from the apprentices, than from the clip on the ear. Still, it taught me to be careful, and, keep a wary eye on Willie's whereabouts. He showed me how to remove the score from the bearing, and then how to sharpen the scraper's edge. He kept his oilstone in a well-oiled, wooden box. It looked ancient, but I made no comment in case I got another clip from his cap. He had also made leather sheaths for his set of hand scrapers. He really looked after his tools, I thought. I had learned a valuable lesson.

The five o'clock hooter blew and I threw my board into the timekeeper's office, and ran for the station. I had a little further to go now, and Belfast Station was closer to the engine works than Ballymacarratt Halt. I showed the guard my 'weekly ticket' at the barrier, got aboard the train and sat down beside James.

'What a day, I am truly knackered and, I have night school tonight,' I said to James as I sat down. 'I enjoyed myself though in the engine works. I am with a wee man called Willie Ross. He is a right nut-case. He hit me with his cap!'

'Oh, they all do that, gives a different meaning to "I take my hat off to you", if you know what I mean,' he laughed. 'I was on the bridge of our ship today; the chippies were laying the wooden deck, and attaching the wheel. Your mob was connecting up the hydraulics. It looks more like a wheelhouse now. I was wiring up the engine room telegraph, the one with all the different segments of glass that light up when you move the brass handle. There is another one in the engine room, which is the same layout and that's how they captain tells the engineer what speed he needs, you know what I mean?'

'Not really,' I replied, 'you lost me a bit, but no doubt I will see it someday.'

Next thing I knew, James was shaking me awake. I must have nodded off.

'I was thinking of getting a motorbike for getting to and from work Willie, my Dad is going with me on Saturday to Tommy Robb's shop in the town. Do you want to tag along?'

'Not half, what sort of bike are you getting?'

'A Honda 125 I think, they are just out, and got a good write-up in the *Motor-cycle News.*'

'Yes, I saw that, and the Hondas are starting to take a few races, are you for the Ulster in a few weeks time?' The Ulster Grand Prix was held at Dundrod in August every year and we saw all the big names such as Phil Read and Mike Hailwood. We had our own Irish riders as well like Tommy Robb, Dick Crieth and Rodney Kinnaird. We got to know the Irish riders quite well, as there were also a lot of local short circuits and road races, throughout the year.

'Had a good day son?' asked Ma as I strolled in through the back door. 'We are having champ and bacon for tea, before you ask. Go and wash your hands.'

I sat down at the table, and Ma put down a feed of champ, that would have kept an army going for months. Champ is made from mashed spuds and chopped scallions (greentails). It was another of my favourites, and along with a glass of buttermilk, filled me up to the gills!

'James is off to Belfast with his Da on Saturday, to buy a new bike!' I said.

'That will cost him,' said Frankie, 'my bike was a year old when I bought it and that cost me nearly fifty quid.'

'I think he has a bit of dough saved up for the deposit, and will pay the rest off on instalments.' I answered.

'Remember you have your test next week William, did you ask your boss for a half day?' Asked Da

'No. I am at day release on Wednesday, but I will ask the teacher tonight for a couple of hours off. It should be okay. Will you do without the bike that day Da?'

'Yes, you can take it to the Tech with you, I will get the lorry driver to pick me up for work, and I don't want to see the L-plates on her when I get home boyo.'

'I hope not, I have swatted the Highway Code for yonks and know it backwards and forwards!' I replied.

'Watch out for the wee man jumping out in front of you during the test. I nearly knocked him down,' said Frankie laughing at the memory.

I ran upstairs to get washed first, while the water was hot. It was hard-going in our house, with everyone going out before seven. I took off on the pushbike towards the college.

'You are going onto the milling machine tonight Scott,' ordered Mr Peden the metalwork instructor. I was at metalwork class.

'Get the bar clamped in the vice, and I will set up the gears with you in a minute.' He went on to give out the others their jobs.

I was to machine a parallel reamer, from bar tool steel as part of the City and Guilds course. This was an examination piece, so I had to be extra careful.

Mr Peden came over as soon as he had got the rest of the lads started, and showed me how to set up the gearing, so that the rotating cutting tool would cut the reamer's flutes at the right angle and speed. I got on quite well with him, as he was an "old boy" of our BB Company, and a friend of my brother Johnny.

'How are you getting on at the yard Willie?' he asked, turning the cooling water towards the cutting tool. This was a mixture of oil and water, which was called glouter or white water in the yard.

'Oh dead on! I am in the engine works, at the bench fitting, good thing I liked mechie drawing though, as we have to read the blueprints. Some of them are quite hard to read.'

'You will get better at the drawings through time. Did I hear your Johnny was getting married?'

'Yes, in October, Kenny and I are going to be ushers. Tails and all!' Kenny was Jean's brother, and a very good friend He was in the class above me at school, and in the BB. He was his third year at Short's aircraft factory, which was beside Harland's.

'Kenny will be like your brother-in-law then,' he laughed. 'Do you still play football for the BB Willie?'

'Yes, now and then although I am leaving the BBs this year. I have to go and see Pa Brown (we referred to our captain thus). I am not looking forward to that meet!'

'Just tell it as it is, and let him know you will join the old boys, when the night school finishes. That's what a lot of us did, mind you, we were doing four nights a week, in those days and no day release!'

'Thanks Frank. I will do just that this week. He will have to find a new goalie for next season.'

Night school finished; I cycled up the road on my own. It was getting colder at nights again. Soon be the 31st September, start of the shooting season again, I thought.

Mags and Beth were sitting talking about the wedding when I got in, and Beth said she had got a new job in a sweetie shop, called the Peter Pan, it was beside the Tonic Cinema, along from the Tech on Hamilton Road

'I've also got a new boyfriend William, and he has a motorbike, so you should like him!'

'What sort!'

'Oh the bike? Can't remember, but it is a green thing, like our Frankie's.'

What are girls like I thought – green thing indeed!

'Are you bringing him to meet Ma and Da soon?' I asked, hoping that I would get to see his bike.

'All in good time, I have only been out with him a couple of times, give us a chance,' replied Beth.

I have your piece ready Child, (she often called me that as I was the youngest) interrupted Mags, 'but no buns now that Beth's not working in the cake shop.' My face fell. 'Don't worry, I start the cookery course in September, so I should get to bring a few fancies home.'

I said goodnight to the sisters, and headed up to bed. I was knackered. I wondered what my Da would saw if I told him that my journey man had clipped me one. Probably would say I deserved it and it would save him giving me one!

Chapter 14

MORE BIKES

On Saturday I went with James and his Da to Tommy Robb's shop in Belfast. It was coming down in buckets as we stopped outside to admire the second-hand bikes. There were a few big Triumphs, Nortons and an AJS on their stands on the pavement, sporting price tags of over a hundred quid. A lot of dough right enough, I thought as we went into the shop.

A wee man in a brown coat came over to James and asked him if he had a bike in mind.

'That red Honda 125 twin,' said James, pointing to the brand new, gleaming Jap machine.

'How much deposit do you need,' asked his Da.

I walked away at this point and let them do their business in private. I was fair jealous, mind you, James was getting a brand-new bike, and he hadn't even passed his test! I looked at some of the other bikes in the shop and quite fancied a second hand BSA C15. This was a 250cc bike, and ideal to fly about on and of course, back and forward to work, a snip at seventy quid marked on the sign beside it.

James's Da took the Honda out for a run.

'He can't half go on the bike James,' I said, watching his Da take off up the street.

'Aye, he used to have an old BSA single, but that was before I was born.' He arrived back and told us that it went great, a bit hard to get used to the gears, them being on the opposite side to his old Biza.

James went over and chose a skidlid and gloves and I watched them ride off, James on the pillion. I had a bit of crack with the salesman, getting the terms for the C15 and headed of down the road to Smithfield Market, which was always worth a visit.

I got Ma a new whistling kettle for a bob. Our old one had a leak, and was always boiling dry, or putting out the gas. I also got myself a brass tea-sugar tin, and a tea can, as I was going to start taking my piece at the bench, with Willie and Effie.

I jumped on a bus up to the Royal Hospital as Effie had asked me to visit his boy Jacky, who was still in hospital.

'Could I see Jacky Marshall?' I asked the nurse at the front of the men's ward.

'Visiting hours isn't till two,' she replied, then relented as I said I had come the whole way from Bangor, especially to see him. 'That's Jacky in that bed over there, the one with all the ropes and pulleys.'

I stopped beside his bed. He was dozing, and I didn't know whether or not to waken him. He was quite big looking, with black hair. He woke up to me staring at him.

'Hi Jacky, I'm Willie. I work at the yard. Effie asked me to pop in and see how you were getting on,' I ventured, answering his bewildered stare. 'I bought you a *Motorcycle News* to read.'

'Thanks Willie, you gave me a start then. What time is it?'

'About twelve, I was up in town, so I thought I would pop up to see you. My mate just bought a Honda 125 out of Tommy Robb's.'

'They are all the rage now, and go like the clappers, for their size. One of my old hands has one and all.'

'How did your bike fare.'

'Oh, a lot better than me, it had crash barriers fitted, so they took most of the crash, I think. My Ma goes off the head if I mention the bike. It is a 650 Road Rocket twin, goes like blazes. I can't wait to get back on her again. Have you a bike Willie?'

'No,' I replied, 'but I am saving up for the deposit. I saw a nice wee BSA in Tommy's this morning. It is going to take forever though; I am just starting my second year. Willie Ross is my journeyman; he is sharing me with Effie, until you get back to work.'

'They are no bad, them two; I shouldn't be much longer in here. I get the plasters off and the pins out next week. A few weeks' physio and I'll be good as new. I was lucky I had my helmet on, mind you or I would have croaked it.' he said laughing. 'Most of these guys in this ward have come off the bikes,' he added, sweeping the ward with his good arm. 'I am looking forward to getting out for the Ulster.'

Just at that Jacky's dinner arrived and I said goodbye, promising to check on him if I was in town next week. Failing that I would see him back in the yard.

He is very brave I thought, sitting on the bus back to town, wanting to get back on his bike after the crash, and, having been tied up to those ropes and pulleys and, with the pins in his legs and all!

The week passed pretty quickly and soon it was Wednesday I was heading out to Newtownards on Da's bike, to sit the dreaded test. I was very nervous as I walked into the test instructors' building.

'William Scott, here to sit a motorbike test,' the receptionist repeated to someone behind her, and out came a man in a bright blue waterproof coat and flat cap. (I found out later why he wore a bright coloured coat!)

Right Mr Scott, can you read that car's mumber plate, ' he asked, pointing to a burgundy Morris Minor, parked about fifty yards away.

I rattled of the number and walked beside him over to the bike; where he checked the L-plates, tyres, tax disc and my provisional driving licence.

'Been learning to ride very long then?'

'About six months,' I replied shakily. I never told him the bike belonged to Da.

'Okay then, start up your machine and ride up to that road junction. Turn left and ride around the square twice. Turn right then onto the main road, then about a hundred yards further along the main road, turn left. This will bring you back onto this street. Pull up at the centre. Repeat this a second time and wait here for me.'

I took all this in and started up the bike, riding up to the junction and onto the Market Square.

Oh No! Here was the market in full swing, cows, sheep, ducks and chickens and stalls, all over the shop!

I rode carefully round them, and completed my first circuit without mishap. I had just started the second lap, when, out from behind a stall jumped the examiner.

'Stop!' He ordered, holding up his hand, palm towards me.

I nearly had a fit; I didn't expect him so soon. I pulled on the front brake, back pedalling to operate the rear one and ground to a good straight stop, without skidding or falling on my face and managing not to stall the engine.

He noted something on his clipboard and to the applause of the farmers, shot off towards the main road. I completed the rest of the test route and stopped the bike outside the test centre.

'Right Mr Scott, a few questions and we are through.' said the examiner.

He asked me about a dozen questions, which I answered parrot fashion, and asked me to step into the office again.

'Well done, you have passed,' he said as he handed me the slip.

'Thank you sir,' I replied unbelievingly. I went outside and ceremoniously ripped off the L-plates and started off for home.

I burst into the house shouting for my Ma, but there was no one at home. I looked out the back door, and saw Granny Ferguson, hanging up her washing.

'I passed my test,' I shouted to her.

'Good boy,' she replied, 'your Ma will be chuffed, she told me this morning that you were sitting your test in Ards. Was it very hard William?'

'Piece of cake!' I replied cockily.

I went back outside and headed back to the Tech. The boys would be surprised, I thought. Poor old Derek though, he failed his a month ago. The examiner had told him he was reckless and going too fast. I wondered how he would have coped on market day!

Chapter 15

BELFAST TOWN

Jacky was back at work, and we had our piece together at the bench.

'I am stripping the bike down this weekend Willie, do you want to come up on Saturday and give me a hand.'

'Sure Jacky, how do I get to your house?

'I live on the Shankill, have you ever been up there?'

'No, I replied, can I get a bus from the City Hall?'

He said he would meet me at the train station, and walk up together, as he needed the exercise. He still had a bit of a limp but otherwise was none the worse for the spill.

We went for a walk round the engine works as soon as we had our piece. Jacky knew a lot of lads our age. We were passing the washer cage, the name given to the metal testing bay, when George came running out.

'What about you Willie, how's the old leg now Jacky?'

'Coming on okay George, still got a bit of gravel rash.' replied Jacky.

'Dead on George, we are going for a wander, coming along?' I invited.

'Naw, got a card school going in there,' he replied, pointing into the bay.

Jacky and I walked on and I nodded to a couple of the lads I was in the training centre with.

'Ever go dancing Willie?' asked Jacky. 'We all go to Romano's on Saturday night, why don't you come along, and stay over at ours, if you like.'

'I don't think so Jacky, I have never been to a dance, and I would need a suit, as I only have a blazer and grey flannels.' I replied.

'Aw well, another time then, George usually goes so you would know a couple of us anyway, you could take my wee sister, she enjoys the dancing. You'll meet her on Saturday – a right tomboy – loves the bikes.'

The horn blew as we arrived back at the benches, Willie and Effie just coming back to life, from the land of nod, as usual.

I was fitting bushes to shafts again today, and getting the hang of it at last, when Willie came over to me.

'Don't look round, but there is the rate-fixer coming our way. I told him you were very slow, and he upped the rate on the governors, for a while. It's been two months since then, so he will time you to see how fast you are now. Take it very canny, we have to bluff him for a few more weeks. I'll keep the extra ones you do in the back of the book for Christmas.'

The rate-fixers (known as rat-catchers) timed your work, and set the rate for each component. Willie kept the numbers of the components in his wee book, and then on a Friday morning would disappear to the bogs for half an hour, and do our books. We got paid correspondingly, so the more we did, the better we were paid, but if we booked in too many, the rate-fixer would cut the rate.

'I am here to time you fitting these bushes to the shafts,' he said.

I looked up and there he was, cream dustcoat, bowler, clipboard and stop watch.

'Dead on,' I replied and picked up a particularly bad looking bush, and a newly machined shaft.

'Where are you off to?' he asked, as I walked away.

'Off to get the key steel, I only get enough to do one job.'

I returned and saw him talking to Willie, whilst keeping an eye on his watch, and started measuring up and marking off the key.

'That's the second time you have checked that! There is no need for that.'

'Every need as you well know Arthur, not so long ago since you were on the tools yourself, forgotten already? Yon bowler gone to your head?' quipped Willie.

Arthur scowled and sat on the bench, continuing to watch my every move.

He nearly blew a gasket when I stopped again to sharpen the scraper, before I started to fit the bush. I took my time and got Willie to check the scraper, wiped his stone with the oily rag a couple of times, and put it back in his locker. I continued to scrape the bearing after I had fitted the key, finishing with a flourish and Arthur stopped his watch.

'Don't know how you make money with this boy,' he said to Willie, as Effie gave me a wide grin behind his back.

'It's hard going right enough Arthur, but I have to train the boy right, it's not all about making money.' replied Willie.

'Humph, you are never short of a bob or two Willie Ross, but the rate stays the same for another month. I will expect the usual Black Bush (Bushmills whisky) on Saturday at the Legion,' he said walking away.

'Well done Billy (he had started calling me Billy as there were four Willies on our side of the shop) I will see you get an extra few bob this week in your pay packet!'

Willie sent the two of us over to watch Bertie fitting the cams to those cam-shafts. Wee Ernie had told him to send us over. Wee Ernie was our foreman, and we got on great with him. He was ex-merchant navy engineer, and was due to retire in a few years time. He told us some cracking yarns, about what the girls in Japan did in the strip joints, and the prices of the watches in Singapore, whilst checking our work, of course.

'What about you boys, come to see how the real engineering is done?' joked Bertie. I had seen him on the way to and from the yard. He rode a BMW shaft driven bike. He kept it in great nick. He was a very highly thought of marine fitter, sometimes going on sea-trials with the engine assemblymen.

'Well, this is the camshaft for the fuel pumps. The fuel pumps are supplied with diesel, and pump it under pressure to the fuel valves. They open under this pressure and spray the fuel mist into the cylinder. The piston then compresses this air/fuel mixture and we have combustion. No spark plug needed! Understand?'

'Yes,' we both nodded, I was fascinated that an engine could run without a spark plug.

'The cams are an interference fit, so we shrink the shafts with this liquid CO_2, and slip the cams on, at the right angle. When the shaft returns to normal tempera-ture, the cams are well and truly tight. You have to be careful to get it right first time, as it is very difficult to get them back off again, if you make a balls up'

We thanked Bertie for showing us the cams being fitted and wandered over to our bench.

'You can see all the parts being made for the main engines, and generators, right here in the shop, Ernie will take you both on another tour next week. Now, back to work we have our pay to make!'

Soon it was Saturday, and I met Jacky at the station.

'Fancy a pint in the Station Bar Willie, or is it too early for you?'

'Aye, too soon after breakfast.' I replied. Little did he know that I had only been in a pub once, the time we sold the ducks to the Crawfordsburn Arms.

We walked by the City Hall, and down Royal Avenue, through Corn Market, and up to the Shankill Road. I had never been up town this far, and marvelled at the red, white and blue painted pavements, and the paintings of King Billy on his horse, crossing the Boyne, on the gable-ends of the houses.

'This is our house Willie, but we will go round the back as no-one will be up yet.'

It was half past ten, I would normally have been up for about four or five hours by this time, if I was going out in the boat, or shooting. However I said nothing and followed him round the back entry.

'No Taigs round here Willie; all my family is in the Orange. Are you in it in Bangor?'

'Err, no Jacky, but I am a good Presbyterian,' I replied, hoping I had gave the right answer.

'Ach well, we'll soon get you into the swing of things. Our Lodge is always looking for new members, although I suppose it's a bit far for you to come every week, to the meetings, eh?'

'I suppose so, but I will think it over Jacky.'

We had reached his back gate and he jumped over the fence and unlocked the gate. I walked into the back yard, very different from ours. No back garden for a start, just a bit of rough ground and cinders and a square of concrete with steps leading up to his back door. His bike was under a tarp in the yard. He pulled the tarp off with a flourish and below was a wicked looking machine, albeit a bit dented and twisted.

'She is a beaut Jacky! Hardly a mark on her.'

'Yeah, I took the crash barriers off, as they were scrap. Anyhow, one of the boys in hospital told me when he had his smash, he got his leg jammed between the crash barrier and the cylinders and got crushed and burned badly, and so I think I will leave them off.

We can take her inside the back kitchen, once everybody has had their breakfast, looks like they are up now anyhow.' Pointing to the back window of the house. 'There's my Ma putting the kettle on, come on in Willie,' he invited me.

We went in the back door and his Ma was making the tea. She wore a sort of a floral dressing gown, and had a fag hanging from her top lip, a hairnet on her head.

'This is Willie Ma, the lad from Bangor who visited me at the Royal. We work beside each other.'

'How are you Willie? Away up and get you're Da and our Jean up Jacky. It's nearly eleven. Jean is going into town with me this morning, and I want your Da to do the windies before he goes to the match.'

She told me to sit down, and gave me a cup of tea. She prattled on for a while then Jacky and his Da came into the kitchen together. He was a big man, well made. I could see whom Jacky took after. He wore a vest, with his braces over the top of it.

'What about you Willie? It's a fine name you have there. I wanted to call this one Willie,' he said punching Jacky playfully, 'but herself wouldn't hear of it – named him after her brother. Got to keep them happy, eh?'

'Yes, Mr Marshall, the yard's full of Willies,' I replied.

Jack's Ma let out a shriek of laughter and his Da nearly choked.

'You have a lovely way with the words Willie, lucky Jeannie wasn't here.' Jacky's Da said.

'Someone mention my name? You must be Willie? This eejit of a brother of mine has been banging on about you for weeks. Makes a pleasant change mind you, from talking about bikes and the Orange Lodge!' she said.

I looked up and there stood Jean. She was a vision of loveliness, tall, slim, with long hair and just a bit of make-up, like Sandy Shaw, I thought! If this were our house, the sisters would not look like this first thing.

'How are you Jean, yes I'm Willie.' I said slowly.

'You didn't tell us he was posh, our Jacky!' she replied

'Och, that's because he is nervous and comes from out of town. They all talk like that in Bangor.' said Jacky.

Jacky's Ma called her away to help with the breakfast, and his Da was coughing like mad, dragging on his first Woodbine of the day. We sat down to a powerful breakfast, bacon, eggs, potato and soda bread and wheaten bread and butter. I had about three cups of tea. His Ma's tea was something else.

'That was really nice, Mrs Marshall, thank you very much.'

'You are very welcome son, nice to be appreciated. This lot take me for granted.'

I excused myself and left the table with Jacky, going out the back door to the yard.

'Give me a push into the side of the yard with the bike Willie, would you? We can start stripping her down out here, and then move into the kitchen when it is clear.'

'Sure Jacky, where do you want to start, will I take the exhausts and silencers off? I have cleaned these before.'

'Dead on Willie, I will leave you to it. I'll get the front wheel off. I will need to get this into Arty's to get it checked and straightened.'

I took of both silencers, and laid them out on a couple of old sacks. One was quite badly dented, and there was not a lot we could do with it. It would probably work okay, but the dents would spoil the look of the bike.

I said as much to Jacky, but he didn't seem too bothered about it and gave me out an old bucket of paraffin oil, to clean out the baffles. We worked away in whistling or joining in to Dusty's new single blasting out from Radio Caroline, on Jacky's trannie.

'Is that all the family Jacky?' I asked innocently.

'You don't know then?'

'Know what Jacky?'

'I have a brother in the Crum (Crumlin Road Prison). He took out a couple of IRA sympathisers about three years ago. We don't mention it much, Ma has had a bad time over it, taking lots of tablets, and the old man has aged about ten years.'

'Hell's teeth Jacky, it must be awful for you all, I am really sorry, we don't know the half of it, down in Bangor.' I replied

Just at that the back gate opened, and George came into the yard.

'How's it hanging boys? Where is the beautiful Jeannie, Jacko?' he asked, making me a wee bit jealous.

'Away to town with Ma. The old man's in, if you want a word with him,' he replied.

George rattled the back door and went into the house.

'Him and the old man are as thick as thieves, goes to the Lodge and football matches with him.' I didn't need to ask which team they supported!

I carried on stripping the silencers and then started to take the chain of, as Jacky wanted the back wheel checked as well.

'Who does the wheels Jacky?'

'Arty, a wee man in the garage at he end of the road, he does bikes and lawnmowers and small engines for boats.'

'I have the back one ready for checking, but it looks all right to me,' I said, spinning the wheel, holding onto the axle.'

'Come on and we will take them both down there now, and when we come back we can lift the heads off her.'

We had a cup of tea and a fag then got started back into the bike, lifting of the cylinder head, complete with rockers and valves. This was the first overhead valve engine I had worked on, as our old track bike was a side valve and my Das bike was a two stroke, with no valves.

Jacky showed me how to compress the valve springs and remove the valves. He marked the valves so we could match them when we were ready to grind them in. We left the barrels on the block, covering them up with a clean rag and then putting the tarp back over the whole bike. I was grinding in the valves, when Jean re-appeared, and putting the kettle on she said,

'How's it coming on boys, look at the state of our kitchen floor, Ma will go berserk if she sees it like that. Lucky we met Auntie May at the shops, so she is away to hers for the rest of the day. She asked me to make the tea. Fancy anything special Willie, or fish and chips from the chippie, across the road be all right?'

'Fish and chips would be dead on, wait a minute and I will come with you,' I replied.

I hastily washed my hands and gave Jacky a hand to tidy up the bike parts, and walked across the road with Jean, leaving Jacky to clean the kitchen lino. She is really very beautiful, I thought, stealing a wee look sideways.

'And what are you looking at Willie Scott from Bangor?' she giggled wickedly.

'Oh nothing, I was looking at the paintings on that wall.'

'Really, and have you not seen paintings on gable ends before?'

'Not until today,' I replied, opening the chippie door for her, and letting out the delicious aroma of fish and chips escape onto the Shankill Road.

'What are you for Willie,' she asked.

'Supper please, but let me get these, I have been eating your Ma and Da out of house home all day.'

'Thanks Willie, very nice of you to offer, I 'm sure, but Ma gave me the money for the tea'

I couldn't tell if she was taking the Mick, or not so she ordered up three suppers, and paid the woman behind the counter.

'Right one you have there Jean,' giving her a big wink, and the thumbs up sign.

'Come on Willie, Jacky will be starving, cheerio Haze,' she said as we left the shop. 'Right nosey cow her, knows everything and everybody on our street, she will be telling everyone that I have a new boyfriend,' she laughed.

We ate our suppers straight from the newspaper wrappings, with lashings of tea, bread and butter. The fish was great, but the chips a bit greasy, like Greasy Joe's, our local chippy in Bangor.

'You staying over tonight Willie? Jacky was saying you might come to the dance at the Orange Hall. Friday night is for the old fogies, but Saturday night we usually have a show-band. They are very good and play all the latest hits.' asked Jeannie, blowing on her chips.

'Not this time Jean, I have to get back home tonight as I am have to sort my Uncle's boat tomorrow morning. He doesn't fish on Sundays, but he will need it first thing on Monday,' I lied. Uncle Jimmy would have a fit if I worked on the boat on a Sunday, but I couldn't very well tell her that I had no suit to wear!

She seemed to be a bit disappointed, but cheered up with the arrival of George and her Da.

'We had fish suppers, you two, do you want me to go over and get a couple?' she asked.

'No love, we are fine, we had a bite at the pub,' replied her Da.

I said my goodbyes and went out the front door. George and Jacky walked me to the end of the road.

'You okay from here Willie?' asked Jacky.

'Aye, no bother boys; I will see you on Monday. Thanks for a great day, Jacky, thank your Ma as well.' I said as we parted.

I made my way back through town to the railway station and jumped onto a train, just as the last whistle was blowing, shouting "weekly" to the porter as I ran through the barrier.

I got up home about eight to see a strange bike in the front of our house. I went inside and Beth introduced me to Cecil, her new boyfriend.

'Hi Cecil, mind if I take a look at your bike?'

'Not at all, come on and I will go out with you,' he replied

'You have passed your test haven't you William?'

'Yes, just last week.'

'Ever ridden one of these?' he asked, patting the Francis Barnett (known as a fanny B!)

'No but I have ridden a James, something like it?'

'I will give you a shot sometime, but not with everyone looking out of the window, I don't think your Ma would like it.'

I liked him instantly, and walked back up the path with him.

'Going to the Ulster next Saturday?' he asked.

'Yes, I was going with my mate, but his Da won't let him take his bike, so we are going with his Uncle in his car.' I replied.

'You can come behind me if you like. Have you got a crash helmet?'

'No, I replied disappointedly.

'Never mind, you can borrow the one Beth uses, if she doesn't mind.

I ran in ahead of Cecil, and asked Beth about her helmet, letting out a whoop, when she said I could borrow it. She said she was working on Saturday and couldn't make the race, muttering something about her hair that I didn't quite catch!

I went up to big Noel's house and had a couple of games of snooker, his Ma and Da were out, so we had a fly fag, and a bottle of his Da's beer between us. I told Noel about my day in Belfast, and he agreed with me that they were all mad up there, shooting each other. However it wasn't long before my Da's prediction came true, and they were all fighting with each other.

Chapter 16

A TESTING TIME

I left Willie Ross with a heavy heart, but I wasn't going very far, just about 600 yards up the shop to the Test House in Bay 3. In here they tested the strength of materials, of which I knew very little!

Big Eddie was still the head foreman, but we got a new general foreman called Alfie Nixon. He was a stocky man, with a very coarse voice, which added to his Belfast accent, but was another star!

'Right boy, Ernie has had a word with me about you, so keep going the same way in here and you and I will get along just fine,' he said as we walked over to my new journeyman.

'This is Billy Scott Tony, he was with Willie Ross the last six months, so should have the rough edges rubbed off by now,' he said, introducing me to Tony.

'Pleased to meet you Tony,' I said holding out my hand. He shook it briefly and told me to go over and stand beside the lathe. There was a man on the lathe, a lot older than Tony, must have been near retirement, I thought. I found out later that he was forty, very old to me indeed.

'You the new boy?' he asked, not taking his eye of the work in the chuck.

'Yes, I'm Billy Scott. Am I the only apprentice in here?'

'Aye, there is only the three of us Tony, yourself and me. The bowler comes in now and then to keep an eye on things, but normally leaves us to our own devices. I'm Andy. Do you play poker or pontoon?'

'Naw, no interest in cards, saving up for a bike,' I answered as Tony came over to us.

'Well Billy, better get you started, come on over here and I will show you the record book.'

He opened a large foolscap book, with lots of figures in about four columns.
'We test all the engine parts castings. When they are cast, they cast a few samples with the main cast. We log the cast numbers in the book, machine the castings and then test them for strength and ductility. Ever done any of this Billy?' he asked hopefully. He was very busy and looked like he could do with a hand.

'A bit of theory, but I am looking forward to the tests. This should make it a bit clearer. I was a bit iffy at the theory.'

'We all were, I have been in here for about eight years, and am still learning. What year are you in?'

'Coming up to my second – well a year and six months. How long will I be here?' I asked

'About six months is usual, but you can ask for a shift after three, if you get bored,' he replied.

'I am sure I won't get bored, I like all types of machines, and need to learn about the strength of materials for the City and Guilds.'

'Good, but see how you like it first, before making up your mind. Most of the apprentices can't get away fast enough!'

He showed me round the wee shop. It was boarded off from the main shop and the washer cage next door. He explained this was because there was a danger of bits of metal breaking under stress and flying about.

'Make sure you always wear the eye goggles. They are a bit of a pain, but a lad almost lost the sight of one eye a while ago, so now we are doubly careful, even when setting up. Belts and braces, Eh?'

We walked over to a tall machine, with a vice at the floor, and a vice like chuck, hanging down from what looked like a tailstock of a lathe.

'See the pieces, like dumbbells that Andy is turning on the lathe? Well, we mark the shaft with two dabs, at a set distance, and clamp one end in each vice.'

'We then stretch the piece, noting the distance apart the two dabs are, just before sample breaks. This dimension is written against the cast number in the logbook, under elongation, and we start the next test, which is to analyse the material. We drill into the cast, and send the cuttings over to the lab. They carry out the analysis and give us back the results, and yes, this goes into the book!'

We went from machine to machine, all having different means to test the samples. I marvelled at the complexity of these tests, and wondered how necessary they were. I asked Tony this question.

'Very, very important; large stresses are put on the components of an engine, and we have to prove that the material will stand up to these. Like the pressure inside a cylinder, when the engine fires. There is pressure on the piston, rings, liner and head, not to mention the crankshafts, hold-down studs and nuts on the tie rods!'

'Never thought of that,' I answered, immediately taking more interest in the proceedings.

We finished up at the Brinell Hardness testing machine, which was a small hydraulic press. The sample was held in the vice and a round-nosed ram lowered onto it. A set pressure was applied and this left a small indentation in the sample. This indentation was measured, using a calibrated magnifying glass. Tables were then consulted and the result entered into the logbook, this time under hardness number.

I had done this in theory and it would be good to be able to tell the teacher at the next night school, that I had actually carried out the test.

The horn blew for lunch, and I took Tony and Andy's can, along with my own down to the hot water sinks.

'What about you Willie, where are you now,' asked Jacky as he filled his tea cans.

'In the Test House, do you know Tony?' I asked innocently. His face clouded and he just nodded.

'See you later,' he said and walked away, talking to one of his mates, and looking back towards me. I heard the word Taig mentioned, but thought nothing of it.

I made the tea, and took the bottle of milk out of my lunchbox. It was an old Camp Coffee bottle, and after topping up my can, handed it over to Tony and Andy.

'Help yourselves, I have plenty.'

'Thanks Billy, is it Bangor you are from?' asked Tony.

'Yes, I get the train back and forward just now, but I am saving up for a bike. I am seventeen this month, so I should be able to get HP sorted out.'

'You would be better to get a cheaper bike for cash, these HP guys rip you off,' said Andy. We got a new suite for the living room over three years ago. It's done, but we are still paying it off!'

'Right enough, but I can't save much once I give my Ma a few bob and pay the weekly train fare. Still I should be getting a rise soon.'

'That's one good thing about working in here, we get a good rate, as it is very important work, and we can't rush it for piece work,' said Tony.

'That's great, I replied.

In fact come Friday, I had about twice my normal wage. Willie had booked a lot of jobs to me and I was well pleased. I went down to see him on Monday and thanked him.

'Did you wake me up for that?' he said when I spoke to him, but I could see he was pleased.

'Thought that would help get you one of those confounded motorbikes; I know you won't rest till you have one. It's your Ma and Da I pity,' he laughed. 'You should see the new boy I got today,'

'A right gawk I bet,' I ventured.

'Indeed not, I was just saying to Effie that I would be able to take it easy now I had a boy who could work fast, and not dawdle about!'

'Don't listen to him Billy, he was telling the new boy that he would never be as good as his old boy,' shouted Effie.

I left them laughing and went back into our shop. Tony was talking to Andy, but stopped as I came up. I thought they were talking about me! But Tony started to talk about the football on Saturday, so I walked away and set up the machine for another test.

My first week's wages from the test house were astronomical; almost a tenner. Once I gave my Ma a fiver and paid the train, I had three quid left over. This was indeed a fortune.

An even bigger surprise awaited me on my birthday. I knew something was going on as Cecil and Ma and Da had been in cahoots about something all week. I came home, and there in the back garden was a motorbike. It was a single, with a green frame, and a leopard skin seat cover, telescopic front forks and jam pot rear suspension. She was old, but in very good nick!

I ran into the house and everyone jumped up and wished me a happy birthday.

'Your Ma and me got you the bike William, it's not very grand, and we can't get it to go, but I am sure you and Cecil will be able to fix it up,' said Da hopefully.

I couldn't believe it – a bike of my own. I couldn't care less if it was going or not. I would soon have her buzzing!

I thanked Ma and Da. Cecil gave me a white scarf, the rest of the family had clubbed together and bought me a crash helmet and a pair of gauntlets. I was on top of the world. No night school for me tonight, I thought, but Da soon put the clobbers on that saying that he would take the bike back, if I started missing night school.

I rushed home from night school and Cecil joined me in the shed. The bike was an Ariel Colt, a 200cc single cylinder four stroke. We tried the spark and fuel and everything looked fine, although the spark was a bit weak. Cecil suggested we pushed it up the back lane and tried a push-start, much to Beth's disgust, as she had been quite comfortable in the kitchen, sitting on Cecil's knee.

We pushed it up and down the back lane and in the end had to admit defeat; she had no notion!

'We will have another look at it at the weekend William, I am sure there is nothing seriously wrong with it. We will soon get it going,' said Cecil confidently.

The weekend came and Cecil had to work, however, I had asked George to stay over for the weekend to go fishing, but it was bucketing down, so we worked on the bike instead.

'Seem to have enough compression; the spark's a bit weak though George, but she should at least fire! But not a squeak; even when I push her till I am blue in the face.'

'Mmh' said George, 'I wonder if the timing is out?'

He took the spark plug out again, and the valve rocker cover off, and put a pencil down the spark plug hole. He put her in gear then turned the engine over, using the back wheel, until both the inlet and exhaust valves were shut.

'Will you turn the back wheel slowly Willie, whilst I watch the pencil? There, see what I mean, the pencil is right up the barrel, and both valves are still shut. The points are nearly shut, with no notion of opening more. This shouldn't happen; the points should just be starting to open, on the compression stroke. I think! I don't know but I know a man who does! Let's go and phone Jacky, if he is in he will tell us what to do.'

We went up to the phone box, at the top of our street, and phoned Jacky. We were in luck, he was just going out. George told him the problem, and after a few minutes thought, Jacky told him what to try. George explained to me the rudiments of a four-stroke engine and I was slowly getting a hold of it. At the compression stroke, the points should open and then the engine would fire. Our points were almost shut, so this was the problem.

Jacky loosened off the points adjusting screw, and brought her up to almost top dead centre, with the valves shut. He adjusted the point's gap and we put the engine back together. He gave her a prod on the kick-start, and she backfired, nearly breaking his leg. As he hopped about swearing, I had another few tries, but this time there was no response from the engine!

'Ah bollocks to it Willie; any chance of a cup of tea and a fag?'

'No bother, I'll go and put the kettle on, come on and sit by the fire, there's only my sister in.'

'Hi Mags, this is George, we didn't get the bike to go yet, but there are some signs of life,' I joked and told her about George's leg nearly getting broke.

We had a cup of tea and a fag each, sitting at the kitchen table; George drew out the sequence of firing, over and over again.

'Can't understand why she backfired, then nothing. Got it! I bet the plug is soaked wet with petrol. We'll have flooded her!'

Sure enough, when we took out the plug again, it was glistening with petrol, and old carbon deposits. I cleaned the plug, while George re-checked the timing and valve clearances, adjusting both again. I set the plug gap with a piece of fag packet and screwed it back in. Dammed if I didn't cross thread it in my haste, and had to make several more attempts before I got it on the right threads. I tightened it up and tried the kick-start again. She roared into life. Now, you have had to have been through the frustration, disappointment and sheer cussedness that an old engine can dish out, before you can have deep satisfaction of an engine eventually firing, and settling down to a nice low, even purr!

'She sounds great Willie, take her out and I will follow on the Goldie.'

I wheeled her out of the shed and jumped on, easing her out past the garden gate and up the back lane. I went out onto Belfast Road, and once clear of the 30mph signs, opened her up. Boy did she go! I looked back and George was coming up fast behind me. He stayed behind me as I turned and headed back home. I hadn't bothered with a coat and I was soaked through but very, very, happy!

There was a surprise waiting for me on Monday morning. Alfie took me to the side and told me I was being shifted to another testing department. This was nothing to do with my work, in fact he was very pleased with me and Tony did not want to lose me. The hydro testing squad (whatever that was!) were a man short, so I had been volunteered to step into the breech! (I wonder who set that up? Someone with the initials ES perhaps!)

The rest of the week went pretty quickly and come Monday I went with Alfie to meet my new foreman, Joe Stitt. Joe took me along to the test bay round the corner in bay 4. In here they tested cylinder liners, cylinder heads and jackets.

'This is your new boy Willie Scott, Kenny,' said Joe introducing me to my new journeyman.

'Thought I was to get a fitter, not a spotty-faced apprentice,' shouted Kenny agitatedly. 'How do you expect me to get through all the work with only a boy helping me?'

'Just give it a try Kenny, he is one of Big Eddies protégées, so he should be okay.'

Just talk among yourselves, I thought. I can do without this, but I was right about one thing!

'Aye okay, sorry lad, I don't mean to go on at you but we are up to our eyes in it!' relented Kenny eventually shaking hands with me. 'Hang your bag and coat beside mine over there and I'll show you around.'

'We test the cylinder heads and liners; then the liners are sent for machining of the scavenge ports, have you ever seen any of these?' he asked pointing to the engine parts.

'Yes, I noticed them a few times when I was walking by your bay. How do you test them?'

'Well, we blank all the openings off and fill them with water. The wee bleed-valve at the top stays open to let the air out, then we close it off and connect the hose and pump to it and bring it slowly to the required pressure. We hold it there for about half and hour and then if there are no leaks, we let the pressure off and start on the next one. Once we have about five or six tested I send for Joe and Mr Atkinson, the DNV Surveyor. Okay so far Billy?'

'Yes, dead on but what is DNV?' I asked.

'That is the surveyor's company, Des Norske Veritas,' he replied 'He comes and witnesses the tests, once we are happy with them.'

I worked away happily, putting in the insertion rubber gaskets and bolting on flanges to the liners and heads. I imagined we had to pressure test the different components to make sure they could stand up to the pressures inside the engine so cooling water didn't get into the engine oil and Kenny verified this when I asked him.

'Aye Billy, water and oil don't mix – always remember that. You said you were going to sea, well, dip your generator and engine sumps regularly, and check for oil. The oil will go "gunnjy" after water mixes with it. Stop the engine right away as the bearings will be shot if there is water in the oil!'

This proved valuable advice and I remembered to carry this out a few years later when at sea. I managed to save a few engines by doing this simple, quick visual check!

Kenny showed me how he wanted the hard stamping carried out. I had to stamp the cast No., pressure tested, and the date of test in a small box, which had been machined for this purpose on the side of the components. I got quite good at this after a while, but not before getting a few clips round the lug-hole with Kenny's cap, as some of the letters were squint!

Mr Atkinson came after a few days and I was introduced to him.

'Pleased to meet you Billy, hear you want to go to sea. I was Chief Engineer with Shell Tankers for about ten years – best years of my life, boy!'

We brought six cylinder liners and two heads up to pressure and he seemed impressed that we had managed so many tests at once for him.

'Well, we work well together, Billy and me, although his stamping leaves a lot to be desired,' said Kenny, and Joe winked at me!

'It is quite hard using these round-nosed stamps. The stamps we used in the training centre were much easier to use,' I ventured.

'Aye well,' replied Mr Atkinson, 'we use round nosed "teeps" because if we use sharp nosed ones, there is a chance of starting off a crack in the metal, as it is under a lot of pressure. Isn't that right Joe?'

'Dead on Mr Atkinson,' replied Joe, looking over at Kenny. Joe told me later that there was an almighty row when Atkinson, as he called the surveyor, found out he was using pointed hard-stamps, or teeps as he called them.

I stayed with Kenny in hydrotesting for a couple of months, making up my total time in testing to six months and then moved into the piston ring department.

Chapter 17

LARGE AND SMALL PISTON RINGS

All too soon again it was time for another shift, this time to the piston ring department.

I was escaping from the evil eye of Big Eddie, or so I thought! Harry Gordon was my new head foreman, but I hadn't met him yet.

George Donaldson, my new foreman brought me to the piston ring department and introduced me to my journeyman.

'This is Billy Scott, your new boy. Billy this is Gerry Smith.'

'Pleased to meet you Billy, managed to escape from the Test House?' asked Gerry.

'Oh, it wasn't too bad, passed pretty quickly, I was supposed to do six months, but got away with four in there, and two in hydro testing,' I replied, looking round the benches.

There were four benches, laid out back to back. There seemed to be an assembly line type of set-up, the rings arriving at one end as complete rings, and then finishing up at the other, all cut and neatly stacked, on wooden pallets.

Gerry introduced me to the other two men in the squad, who were pretty young looking and not long out of their time, by their looks. They hardly took time to shake hands, and they were off again, filing and hacksawing the rings like billio.

'Good piece rate here Billy, everyone pulls their weight and we split the bonus between us,' said Gerry. The rings are machined over there on that hurdy gurdy. The bogy takes them over to us. You are the first stop, come on over to your bench and I will show you what to do.'

He led me over to my bench and stopped beside the vice, which held a wooden wedge that had a vee cut into its top end.

'Your job is to take the burrs off the inside and outside of the rings with a file like this,' gripping a ring and holding it into the vee of the wedge. Then you pass to Harry over there and he saws them at 45 degrees. Next they go to Walter and he files the butts and passes them to me. I size them, using these gauges and mark their size on the inside surface with this electric pen. I pile them up on these pallets, where the inspector checks them before sending them on the bogy to the heat treatment, over there,' he finished.

It seemed straightforward enough. I thought I would be bored stiff. However, the pace was such that when the hooter blew for lunch, I hadn't had time to get bored.

'Give me your cans and I will get the tea,' I said to the men.

'Good lad Billy, you did well this morning, keep up the good work,' Gerry said, just as Big Eddie was passing. He looked over and gave me one of his by now familiar half-winks, falling in beside me, as I made my way to the sinks.

'Well boy, settling in okay? I told Harry Gordon to keep an eye on you and not let you skive off!' He said out of the corner of his mouth.

'Yes thanks Mr Schoffield. Skive in here? You must be joking, they hardly stop for breath! But I really enjoyed the last couple of shifts and think I am going to like it here,' I replied, as he half ran up the stairs to his office in the sky.

I had my tea and went for a wander round my new area. The men had all finished their pieces and were lying sleeping on their benches, or sitting beside the machines, reading the paper. I wandered into the heat treatment department, but did not stay very long. The place stank to high heavens and was very dusty and hot. A furnace door lay open. Inside were our rings, in neat piles on a steel bogie, which ran on rails on the bricks of the furnace floor. There was definitely a terrible smell. I couldn't place it, but the place was reeking!

The horn blew as I came back to my bench, and I picked up another ring and started filing the burrs off the inner and outer edges. I had to be quite careful, even though the pearlite cast iron was pretty hard; I only had to put a chamfer of about a sixteenth of an inch around the outside and the inside of the rings. This was to remove the small burrs and rough edges. I then gave the rims a quick rub with emery cloth. I wore a pair of working gloves, as the edges were very sharp from where the hurdy-gurdy man had parted them from the machined cylinder.

The hooter blew, announcing the end of the day. It had gone surprisingly fast and as I put away my tools, I mentioned this to Gerry.

'Aye, we are kept going. There is always a rush on for rings, both as spares and for the assembly shop. I will take you over there sometime and let you see your rings being fitted to the pistons. They are sample liners that I use to size the rings,' he said pointing to a couple of small cylinders beside his bench. 'I use that smaller cylinder for sizing the generator piston rings,' he continued, as we walked towards the door of the engine works.

'I will see you tomorrow Billy, I have to run and catch the bus, and you're from Bangor aren't you? Do you get the train?'

'No,' I answered proudly, 'I have a motorbike over there in the sheds. See you tomorrow Gerry.' I shouted as I reached the bike and got my helmet and gloves out of the carrier on the back.

She started first kick. In fact she never missed a beat. Cecil had helped me overhaul the engine. We had ground in the valves, fitted new springs, polished the inlet and exhaust ports and splashed out on a new spark plug. I got out onto the main road and as I accelerated by a crowded bus, I looked in through the window and waved at Willie Ross. He just shook his head as I disappeared in a cloud of exhaust smoke, nearly coming a cropper on the tramlines. It only took about fifteen minutes to get to Bangor since the new by-pass had opened up.

I loved the devil's elbow, a particularly nasty bend near Cultra, but slowed up at the next big one at Ballysallagh turn off, where our Frankie had come off his bike last year. He was unhurt and badly shaken although the piano innards frame that he had strapped to his back didn't fare so well. No amount of his putrid horse-hoof glue would fix this baby!

The next day at work Gerry had shown me how to deburr the oil rings. These were different from the compression rings.

'See all the wee holes bored around the circumference Billy, use this rat-tail file to get all the burrs off. These rings scrape the excess oil from the cylinders. The oil goes through these wee holes and runs back down into the sump. What do you think would happen if we didn't remove the burrs?'

'Well, I suppose the oil wouldn't get through the holes so easily, and the burr might scratch the cylinder, or fall into the sump if it came off.' I answered.

'Good, so take your time and be extra careful with these rings. Have you worked on many engines Billy?'

'Yes, mostly motorbike engines though, nothing this size,' I replied spanning the ring with my arms.

'Don't matter, cleanliness is essential in any engine, a piece of metal or bit of dirt in the lube system can drastically reduce the life of an engine.'

I carried on by myself then, deburring the edges and then the oil holes in the rings, passing them on down the line. I had got through a lot when Gerry and Ernie came over to my bench.

'Ernie is going to take you for a walk round the heat treatment and maybe down to the piston bay,' he said. 'Don't be all day!'

'Never mind him Billy; you will soon make up for the time lost. This is part of your training, you know. George asked me to show you round as he has a lot on today. Harry is like Big Eddie, he wants to give his boys the best training, and I help as much as I can. We will start over there at the heat treatment.'

We walked into the furnaces area and the place was still reeking, and hot as hell. 'What is that smell Ernie? I asked, 'It was stinking the last day I was here as well.'

'That will be the cyanide they use to case harden the bottom of the compression rings. When the engine fires, the gas presses against the top of the compression rings, pushing them hard down onto the bottom of piston groove. This causes the ring to wear badly at the bottom, and it could eventually go squint. We harden the bottom edge of the compression rings to prevent them wearing,' he explained.

I did like Ernie, he knew about everything concerning the engines, through all the different stages of machining and assembly. He never laughed if I asked a stupid question, and looking back, I must have asked a few crackers!

'Come on down the shop a bit and I will show you where the rings get fitted to the pistons. After they leave the heat treatment area, they are taken down to the piston department,' he explained, as we passed the longest lathe I had ever seen which was turning out a large crankshaft about 30 foot long!

We stopped at the pistons assembly area, and I looked around. There was a stack of pistons, blocked up with wooded wedges and staging. Beside the pistons were large cylinders. The cylinders had a row of slots machined about a third of the way up. Ernie explained that these cylinders were the diesel engine cylinder liners, and the slots were the air inlets in the Burmeister & Wain two-stroke engine.

The liners would be match-fitted to the piston and rings. The rings were first thoroughly cleaned and oiled. They were then slid into the cylinder and the gap between the butts checked. The rings were then expanded using a screwed clamp, which allowed them to be lifted over the piston and fitted to the grooves. There were four compression rings and two oil rings, per piston.

I was fascinated and could have spent all day here, just watching and drinking in the experience. This was what I had longed for. How fortunate I was to see all this first hand. As it was it stood me in very good stead later on at sea, as the first ship I sailed on had a Kincaid Burmeister and Wain two-stroke diesel engine as her main propulsion unit! Identical to the one I was seeing assembled.

I was brought back to the present by Ernie shaking my shoulder and telling me to make my own way back to the department, as he had to go elsewhere. I stayed and watched for a few more minutes, the men trial-fitting the rings, then fitting them to the pistons and pairing the pistons with their liners. I noticed a ring of small holes drilled round the cylinders and made a note in my book to ask Gerry or Ernie what they were for. I had been keeping a journal, since leaving the training school, updating it at lunchtime.

I returned to the bench and nodded over to Gerry, one of the other men looked pointedly at his watch and back at Gerry, who just shook his head. I started back to work and soon had a stack of finished rings ready to pass onto Harry. That will keep the ol' bugger busy for a while, I thought.

That evening, at night school, the teacher was discussing the strength of materials, and all the tests involved. We had to write an essay on this for next week. I had all the gen neatly tucked away in my wee book! Nice one old son I thought, about time I had a break.

The maths was giving me the boke! We were doing advanced algebra, which I could just about handle. Then along came calculus! Yuct! I could not get a hold of this at all! Differentiation! Functions! What is this all about?

I was at my wits end and only brother Johnny saved me from going batty. He sat down one night and explained the fundamentals to me. I still didn't understand what calculus was used for, and had no idea if I would ever need it, but with Johnny's help I managed a pass of forty five percent later that year! (After forty years in marine engineering and offshore oilrigs, I still haven't used calculus!)

I called into Toni's café on the way home and ran into George and Derek. They were discussing the merits of singles versus twins, the usual crack. I got a coffee and sat down beside them. There were a couple of new records in the jukebox, and I went over to have a look. I was right into Jim Reeves, Dusty, The Bachelors and The Seekers. The Beatles were starting to forge ahead on the hit parade, and nearly every record they brought out was a hit. I also liked Gerry and the Pacemakers and the Dave Clarke Five. Mags and I were slowly building up a collection of records that what turned out to be in the best music decade of the century. (Or maybe I am just hooked on sixties music.) I put a tanner in the slot, picked a couple of Dusty's 45s and sat down again lighting a fag.

'How's work Derek, you must be nearly out of your time now,' I asked.

'Work's fine, I am in my last year, well just started it really, but I passed the City and Guilds Motor Mechanics course and am finished with the tech; at last!' he replied.

Derek had done really well, much better than I had expected. At school, he never made the Technical College, staying on at the Intermediate School till he went to serve his time in a local garage. He was very good at the bikes and well respected, his advice often being sought by the rest of us.

He had bought a 350cc Velocette single, and he kept it in great nick, frequently blowing off the opposition of big Triumphs and Nortons. My old thing could hit almost seventy, well – with the wind behind me!

I had put a notice up in Toni's café and on the board at work advertising her for sale for thirty quid! Who knew what I would get for her, but I was after a big twin, and it wasn't very far away!

Chapter 18

THE ASSEMBLY SHOP – BACK UNDER BIG EDDIE'S EYE!

'Remember these two reprobates Bertie? Well, they are all yours for a couple of months – best of luck – you will need it!' said Big Eddie leaving us with Bertie McClure.

I had been shifted to the assembly areas, and had been put with Bertie, along with Jacky!

'Right you two, do you remember what I showed you a few years ago?' asked Bertie.

'It was a wee while ago Bertie, but I am sure we will manage,' answered Jacko, for the both of us.

Bertie started us on a couple of reversing units, one apiece. These were used to reverse the cams and air start mechanism, when changing the engine from ahead to astern. He gave us a drawing and left us to it as he was in the middle of shrinking cams onto shafts for the fuel pumps.

'How's the old Ariel going Billy Boy? asked Jacko.

'Oh, okay, but the clutch is slipping a bit, I'll tell you about it at dinner time as Bertie is watching us.'

We worked away for a couple of hours then Bertie came over to see how we were getting on and helped us out with a few problems.

'Not too bad, boys. Watch how you connect the levers, make sure they are straight before you connect them, and don't try to straighten them once they are connected. I saw you at the hammer there Billy, this is fragile gear and balance is a big part of the mechanism,' he instructed me.

I went and got the tea with Jacko, and we sat down on the bench beside Bertie.

'What were you saying about your clutch Billy?' asked Bertie, as he drank his tea.

'It is starting to slip in first and second, then it is all right in third until I come to a hill or accelerate quickly, then it starts again. I have adjusted the cable and the clutch adjuster at the gearbox as far as they will go.

'Probably need a new clutch. You are cheaper to buy a set of cork inserts and a set of new springs.' Here,' he said, reaching into his locker, 'have a look in the spares section of this *Motor Cycle Mechanics* magazine and see if there is a supplier for your bike. It's an Ariel, isn't it?'

'Yes,' I said, reaching out for the mag, 'thanks Bertie.'

I sat down on the workshop floor, with Jacko beside me and we looked through the spares section. I took down a supplier's telephone number and looking at my watch asked Bertie if I could nip out to the phone for a few minutes.

'Aye go on Billy, but be back before the horn. You know what Big Eddie is like!'

I phoned up the supplier but they told me they no longer supplied cork inserts, only complete replacement clutches. I held my breath as I waited for the price – twelve quid! I asked him about the springs and he told me the length they should be. If mine were within this size, they were okay.

I never got a chance to talk to Bertie the rest of the day. I stripped the clutch down that night at home and measured the pressure plate springs. They were okay; but the corks on the clutch plates themselves were burnt black and very smooth.

I went down to a neighbour's house that night. Harry Thompson lived a few doors down and was a very keen grass-track racer. I had spent a good few nights in his garage working at bike engines, and rattled at the garage door.

'Hi William, come on in it is freezing out there.'

'How's it going Harry? What about you Gordy?' I greeted him and his mate.

They were stripping down the grass-tracker's gearbox. The engine was a 500cc, long stroke JAP single, and she ran on dope, going like a bat out of hell. I enjoyed the grass-track racing, as it was much like the speedway on the telly.

'I have a problem with the clutch on my bike Harry, it is slipping and I stripped it and brought it down for you to see,' I said, handing over the offending plates.

'Burnt to buggery!' said Harry, handing them onto Gordy.

'The man's right William – well shot, I'm afraid you will need a new clutch,' verified Gordy.

'I phoned a supplier in Belfast today, but they only do reconditioned ones and don't sell the cork inserts separately, I said. 'If I could get a sheet of cork gasket material, like we have in work, only a lot thicker, do you think I could cut out new corks?'

They both nodded and said they would help if I could get the material. I stayed on for a while, watching them stripping the gearbox and listening to their crack, as they found the offending stripped gear.

'See this William, this is what happens when you give the JAP big licks and hit a few bumps in the grass at the same time – the gearbox complains, but he doesn't listen,' said Gordy, pointing at Harry with the stripped cog!

'Away you go you eejit, sure I was leading the whole pack up until then and I wasn't going to let that wee no-mark from Belfast get past me at the last bend,' countered Harry.

'I am away boys; do you think that the clutch will hold out till the weekend, I'll get a weekly for the train then?'

'Aye William, you can't do it any more damage, unless you overheat it and warp a plate. Keep the revs down and you should be okay,' answered Harry.

'Aye William, just like Harry does, I don't think!' shouted Gordy as I shut the door behind me.

I went up the back lane and into our shed. Harry had suggested giving the corks a bit of a rub with rough sandpaper, to give them a better grip. After I did this I rebuilt the clutch and went into the house. I was freezing!

'Cup of tea on child,' said Mags as I came through the back door. She was sitting having her hair done by her friend Joan.

'Thanks Mags, anyone else for a cup?'

'Never known to refuse,' answered Joan. She had been my Sunday school teacher yonks ago, but we got on fine.

I poured out a couple more cups of tea and took mine through to the living room. Ma was knitting and Da was sleeping on the sofa, everyone else was out.

'Did you see Harry about your bike son?'

'Yes Ma, he can't fix it either, looks like I am going to have to put it off the road and save up for a new clutch.'

'How much is it?' she asked

'About twelve quid, but it will be worth it to get her going again. I have about six quid saved up, so I will have the rest in a few weeks' time.'

'Cecil and Beth will be in shortly, ask Cecil if he can help you. He is very good at bikes as well,' said Ma hopefully.

'Och, I don't think he will be able to sort this one. I am off to bed, night all!'

I was lying in bed reading the magazine that Bertie had lent me, and looking at an article on clutches when it hit me! Guinness bottle corks! If I could get a load of these I could cut them to size! I lay awake for a long time thinking about this and the more I thought about it, the more confident that it would work I became.

I talked it over with Bertie and Jacky the next day at lunchtime, and they thought I was mad, and would have to drink about a crate of Guinness before I had enough corks. But I had a better idea, and put it to the test on the way home from work.

'Fit like Wullie, got a few ducks for me?' asked Jimmy, as we stood outside the back door of the Crawfordsburn Inn.

'No Jimmy, I need a really big favour though, is your boss about?'

'No the now, he disn'y start till seven, what's on your mind China?'

'I need about a couple of dozen Guinness bottle corks, unused if possible.'

'Nae bother, old son. Wait there the now!' he said disappearing into the kitchen.

He arrived back, rather breathlessly, a few minutes later carrying a brown paper bag full of corks – unused!

'You are a star Jimmy, thanks a million,' I said as I leapt onto the bike and took off towards home.

I managed to shape a set of corks and, after soaking them overnight fitted them at the weekend. The bike was as good as new and it cost me nought! The clutch was a bit ropey for a few days till it bedded in, but then that was to be expected. Bertie told me to write to the bike magazine, telling them my idea, but I decided to keep it to myself, telling him that I might patent it someday!

Chapter 19

THE BROTHERS GRIM!

Our next move at work was across the bay to the valve-testing department. Two brothers, Brian and James Blair, ran this. Bertie had taken us across on the Friday before we were due to start, so we knew where to go.

'Don't I know you Jacky?' asked one of the brothers. 'Aren't you in the Shankill Lodge?'

'Yes,' replied Jacko, with a grin, 'and youse are both in the Sandy Row lodge! I thought I knew youse from somewhere!'

Oh, no I thought – not three Orangemen together, I would never survive this one!

'What about you Billy?'

'Not him,' replied Jacky, before I could open my mouth, 'although he is a good old prod, aren't you Billy Boy?'

'I suppose so, anything for a quite life,' I ventured.

'Won't be quiet for long if the Fennions get their way they'll have us in the "Free State" before you know it,' said Jamsey.

'Over my dead body!' put in his brother.

Eventually we got to work on a couple of air-start valves. These were bolted onto the cylinder heads and used to force compressed air into the cylinders. This started the engine rotating and then she fired, this all tied in with the reversing gear we had been working at with Bertie. I was grinding in the valve, when Big Eddie materialised; as usual from nowhere.

'Well boy, what are you up to today?'

'Grinding this valve into its seat,' I replied nervously as usual.

'Well make sure you test it thoroughly before we send for the DNV surveyor,' he said seriously.

He went on to tell me about an accident that had occurred on a ship due to a faulty air-start valve. The valve had leaked hot exhaust gas back into the compressed air line and had caused the explosion, killing one engineer, and injuring another. This made me double my efforts when grinding in the valves. Usually I would just use course then fine grinding paste when working on the bike engines; but here we did it properly, starting with course, then medium then fine paste.

When we had finished grinding, we tested the assembled valves by pouring paraffin into the recesses. A dry seat would tell that the valve was seated properly. If the paraffin leaked thro' the valve seat, we carried on grinding!

We also ground in the fuel valves. There were three of these on the cylinder head and they opened under pressure of the fuel pumps. We ground these valves into their seats exactly the same way as the air-start valves. We tested these by pumping fuel oil into the valves and adjusting the settings so that when the fuel pressure reached the required setting, the valve would open with a "squeak", and close again, without dripping any oil.

The last valves were the relief valves. These were a safety valve, which were set to "lift" under excessive cylinder pressures.

Mr Atkinson witnessed a percentage of all the valves. He just turned up and picked a couple of valves at random and asked to see them re-tested. We never had any rejects, and as he came to trust us more and more, his visits become fewer. He told us some crackers about his time with the oil tankers and a real scary one about an explosion in port up the Persian Gulf;

He was on a Shell ship which passed another tanker which had been opened up from stem to stern as if by a tin opener, by an explosion. Only its mast and funnel was visible above the water. The captain told him that he had heard that a junior engineer smoking in the toilet caused the explosion.

When they were loading crude, the only smoking allowed was in the wardroom. This lad had been having a few puffs in the bog and the fumes coming down the air-conditioning had ignited.

'How did they know the boy was smoking; he must have been burnt to a cinder?' Asked Jamsey as if, on cue.

'Aye well, the fag was still in his mouth, burned down to a butt, mind you!' He laughed; then we all laughed. 'Joking aside Billy, if you are ever on tankers, remember to abide by the "No Smoking" rules, it only takes a small naked flame to cause an explosion!' Mr Atkins said, walking away.

Chapter 20

SCRAPING A LIVING

My last shift was to the bearing scraping and engine assembly squads. My journey-man was Charlie Carson. Charlie was another grass-tracker, and had won several cups. His brother Austin had been a champion motorcycle road racer and had been killed in the Isle of Mann TT race.

'Well Billy Boy, hear you like the bikes, what have you got?' asked Charlie as we were introduced.

'An old Ariel Colt,' I replied, 'but I am looking for a twin.' I replied.

He took me over to the bearings, which were laid out on the floor. He showed me how to mix the red-lead and oil mixture, which was smeared scantily onto a mandrill. The mandrill was lowered onto the bearing, rotated and then lifted clear. This left red high-spots on the bearing, which we would scrape off until we achieved a full covering of red-lead markings over the whole bearing.

'We don't want to have a completely unbroken, smooth bearing surface, as there has to be room for the oil to gather between the white metal bearing surface and the crankshaft. Instead of scraping the normal way, we use a different method called hatch-scraping,' instructed Charlie and proceeded to demonstrate this to me.

The bearing was scraped from one side then from the other side, giving a patch-work-quilt-like appearance. Charlie explained that these "pockets" would hold the oil pressure and prevent too much contact of the moving parts.

Next we fitted the top half of the bearing, with the mandrill in between and scraped this half as before. Once he was satisfied with the bearing surfaces, Charlie put three strips of very thin lead wire between the top bearing and the mandrill and then tightened up the bearing bolts.

Once these were loosened and the top half removed the "leads" were measured using a micrometer, and this gave the bearing clearance. If it was excessive, the brass shims between the bearing feet were removed and the operation repeated until the desired setting was achieved.

This was all to stand me in very good stead, later at sea and proved to be another invaluable part of my training. I was told that due to the shortage of trained apprentices on the outfitting berths, it had been decided that I had had thorough enough engine training and after a week in the engine assembly I was to be shifted outside to finish the last few years of my time.

Chapter 21

MY FIRST TWIN

I spent my last week with Charlie, before going into the engine assembly squad, albeit only for a few weeks. Meantime I was looking forward to the weekend as Cecil had told me he had a surprise in store. We had been going to the road races nearly every weekend, and knew all the local boys as we spent a lot of time in the pits. They weren't like the real pits on TV, just a lot of vans and bikes in a field beside the track, or aerodrome, but we picked up a lot of tips from the Aces!

I was cutting the grass in the front garden and heard a snarl of a big twin, coming down our hill. It drew up outside our house and I nearly fainted as Cecil got off it and pulled it onto its stand. I ran up garden path, nearly breaking my neck on the grass rake, in my haste and out the front gate. He was standing beside a brand new Triumph Bonneville. It was grey and dark purple and smelt wonderful.

'You ratbag, why didn't you tell me!' I shouted at him.

'No time, just picked her up this morning, you are the first to see her. Is Beth at work?'

'Yes, I am on my own, start her up again, I love that roar. It beats the sounds of the other bikes hands down.'

He started her up and I sat astride her, giving the throttle a wee twist, and feeling the power between my legs. I switched the engine off and we went into the house.

'How do you like my lid, I painted it up especially for the new bike?' he asked

I looked in wonder at his helmet; he had painted it much the same design as our hero Mike Hailwood's helmet, complete with a transfer of crossed flags.

'It is beaut,' I said, 'are you doing the same with Beth's lid?'

'Probably,' he replied handing me a fag.

We lit up in silence and I looked out of the front window, still marvelling at the Bonnie.

'Was it very dear, Cecil?'

'Just under 300 quid, give or take; I got a good price on my Fanny B. She was a good old bike, never let me down. The Bonnie is a wee bit faster, mind you,' he joked.

A wee bit faster? *The Motorcycle News* had run an article on all the big twins a few weeks ago; the Bonnie was the fastest bike around, nearly a hundred and fifteen; well over the ton!

'Did you open her up yet?'

'No', he replied, 'I have to run her in for a thousand miles, at about fifty or sixty. This gives the rings and bores a chance to smooth off a bit. I won't be long running her in, as I do nearly three hundred miles a week.'

We drank our tea and smoked our fags in silence for a while.

'Coming to the Temple this afternoon?' he asked

'No need to ask, I have been looking forward to the race all week,' I replied. The Templepatrick road race was one of the best of the season. The country roads were closed for the afternoon to allow the race to take place. 'Can I come on the back of you, just to see how she goes?'

'Sure, I would give you a shot, but the insurance only covers me. It was pretty steep at that.'

'That's okay; I wouldn't let anyone else ride my Colt either. I am thinking of flogging her and getting a bigger bike, before the end of the summer. I put a notice on the board at work.'

'Hey! That reminds me, I saw an old Thunderbird up for sale last week. We could go and have a look at her tomorrow, if you like. Any interest in your Ariel?' he said.

'Aye, a man in our area said he would give me thirty quid for her.'

'Thirty quid! We got her for a fiver, from the women your Ma works for, as it wouldn't start and it had been off the road for a long time.'

'So that's where she came from. I will let her go to the man in work, if I like the Thunderbird. How much is it?'

'Well, the advert said that it was ten years old, and the bike had been dropped, so we will wait and see. If it goes okay, we could do her up!'

The Templepatrick road race was super, and I enjoyed riding behind Cecil on his new machine. He arranged to meet me on Sunday, and went off to pick Beth up from work.

We were all finished our tea; a big Saturday night fry-up. I was helping Beth with the dishes and asked her how she liked Cecil's new bike.

'Once I got over the shock it was all right. There was a big crowd around it when Cecil picked me up. It certainly is a lot nicer than that old green thing he used to have.' She replied. Sisters–what are they like? An old green thing indeed, talking about Cecil's old Fanny Bee like that!

We met up the next day, when the rest of the family were at church and I went behind Cecil on his Bonny, to have a look at the Thunderbird. We drew up beside the owner's house, and I walked over to the bike, which was parked outside on the street. She was in a bad way, and hadn't seen a cloth or polish for years.

It had a fibreglass fairing, which was badly damaged, and the silencer on one side dented and the chrome scratched. The headlamp glass was cracked and one end of the handlebars was bent up at an angle. Otherwise she looked sound; no oil leaks on the pavement below her.

The owner came out. He was about thirty and walked with a limp.

'You the one that phoned?' he asked, looking at big Cecil's Bonnie enviously.

'No, I did,' I replied, 'what happened to the bike?'

'Fell off her a few weeks ago, busted my ankle and wrist, so it will be a while before I can ride again. That's if I ever do. I am thinking of getting a car.' He said, kicking the front wheel.

'Mind if I start her up?' I asked

'Here's the key, she might be a bit hard to start, it's been a few weeks since I started her up.'

I turned on the juice, tickling the Amol carb, until the bowl was full. I slid the air filter cover half shut and kicked her into life. She coughed a few times then I cleared her throat. The hackles rose on the back of my neck, at the throaty roar as I blipped the throttle.

'Is it safe enough to try a wee run?' I asked him.

'Sure, my old man took her for a run, while I was in hospital.'

I put her in first and pushing her of the stand with my feet; I looked over my shoulder and took off! She handled quite well, despite the damage and the bits hanging of her. I turned at the top of the road and give her a big lick, slowing as I came back to the house. Cecil was sitting side-saddle on his Bonny with his feet on the footpath, smoking a fag as I drew up at the kerb.

'Where's your man?' I asked.

'Away into the house. He said to come and see him when you were finished trying the bike out.'

We discussed the damage, reckoning that once we got shot of the fairing and straightened the footrest and handlebars, she would be a goer. We talked about a price then and decided to see how much the man wanted for her.

The owner came to the door and invited us in, asking if we wanted a cup of tea. His whole family were looking on so he took us through to the scullery and we sat don to a cup of tea and a fag each.

'How much are you asking for her, I said, bearing in mind I will have to get the frame and wheels checked out?' I asked

'Well, I was thinking about forty-five quid.'

'We will give you thirty quid cash, right now and take her away with us tonight,' replied Cecil, before I could answer.

'Done!' he said, 'cash mind you.'

Cecil peeled three tenners out of his wallet and I got the logbook and a receipt. We went back outside and I climbed aboard the Thunderbird, started her up and took off, Cecil riding very close behind me. We got home and I put her into the shed, and then ran into the house to tell all and sundry that I had a new bike. Everyone was surprised, especially as I had told no one that I was selling the Ariel.

'Well son, I hope you will go easy on that big bike, we bought you the small one for your birthday to learn on, but we hoped you would keep it for a while,' said Ma.

'Ach, I just love that old bike and never forget the surprise youse sprung on me but have almost her sold to a man in work, and then I will pay Cecil back.'

'Will that be okay Cecil? That was good of you to lend the lad the money, I can pay you back a few pounds, if you like,' said Da

'Not at all, Mr Scott, I had a bit left over when I sold my old bike. I will give William a hand with his new one and then he can get it on the road. I can wait till then,' he replied. 'Can we borrow your six-foot level, to check the frame and wheel alignment? I am sure it is fine, but it is better to check it.' He never mentioned that the bike had been in a smash, merely said he had dropped it at a bend.

We went into the shed and pulled off the fairing. We took of the handlebars, straightening them in the shed door, and replacing them on the frame. Then Cecil jumped on the bent footrest a few times retightened the nut and passed it fit for purpose!

Just at that Da came into the shed with his long spirit level, and we placed it along the frame, between the front and back wheels, repeating the exercise on the other side. The frame was in line and the wheels looked okay, but Cecil told me later that I should get them checked by a garage. I knew just the place, the wee garage on the Shankill Road, beside Jacky's.

I had a lot of homework to do for Monday night, so I went up early, thanking Cecil and looking forward to getting the Thunderbird on the road.

A few days later I managed to sell the Ariel to Harry, who worked beside Charlie, getting £30 for her. I brought the logbook into work with me and handed it over to Harry, along with a couple of spares I had collected along the way. It felt strange that night, boarding the train with my lunchbox under one arm and the skidlid under the other.

I got home and was getting washed when Cecil came in and I returned his thirty quid to him.

'Thanks old son, did you get the T bird wheels checked out yet?' He asked pocketing the dough.

'Aye, got them both done for five bob at the garage beside Jacky's. The wee man said the front needed tweaked a bit, but the back was dead on.'

'How well do you know Jacky, William?'

'Oh, pretty well, I have been knocking about with him and George for a good while now. Why do you ask?' I replied, slightly confused.

'Well, you know the fighting in Belfast last weekend; there was a photo of Jacky throwing stones at the peelers. I thought if he was in the Orange, he would support the police,' Cecil said.

'I don't know an awful lot about what they get up to, but I know the police were caught in the middle of a row between Prods and Catholics last week. The men in the yard were talking about it during the week. I stay well clear of all that. George and Jacky were both at me to join their Lodge, but I put them off, and they don't like me being so friendly with one of the Catholics I worked with,' I said remembering his warning some time ago about being too friendly with Tony.

'I had visited Tony's home once, while I was working with him in the Test House. He lived in a predominately Catholic area of Belfast, and his house seemed to be filled with crucifixes.

'It didn't bother me at the time, but looking back it was a bit silly of me. We were not supposed to knock about with Catholics outside work! I was told the time was coming when I would have to choose sides, there was no room for "middle of the road men" in the yard,' I finished.

'True enough William, make your own mind up and pick your friends carefully, the folk in Belfast have different views from us down here, and you must respect them, while you are working in the yard,' said Cecil.

We sat down to dinner and the talk was of a new Woollies opening up on the main street in Bangor, the old one being taken over by a bakery that Cecil's brother Jack worked for.

I liked Cecil a lot and we became good mates, and even closer like brothers when he announced his engagement to Beth. Our family was getting smaller, Frankie and Johnny were married; Robert away at sea. Soon there would be just myself, Mags, Ma and Da!

The next weekend we rebuilt the Thunderbird and with Cecil following me I rode up the Belfast Road, giving her her head as I passed the black and white, no speed limit signs. I took her up through the gears, and she responded beautifully. I held her wide open on a straight and throttled back as the speedo needle stopped at eighty-five! Not bad I thought, for an old girl.

We went back home and I took her into the shed. There was oil flying out of about every gasket on the engine and the exhaust pipes were purple. I sat down beside her and lit a fag, listening to the crackles and pinging of the engine and pipes cooling down. I needed new gaskets, that's for sure. We had thought the old ones would do for a while, but I would never be able to put her on the road in this state.

'You were doing almost ninety old son, saw your back end giving a few wiggles mind you,' said Cecil joining me on the shed floor, 'Why the long face?'

'She is pissing oil out of crankcase, rocker covers and pushrod tubes. No wonder I nearly came off, the back tyre is sodden in oil. There is very little oil left in the tank.' I replied dejectedly.

We sat smoking for a while, and Beth came out of the house.

'Are youse two coming in for a cup of tea, you have been out here all night. Cecil, I never see you at all hardly,' she said, hands on hips.

Oh, Oh, I thought, I better make myself scarce and headed indoors. I had a cup of tea and headed off to my room to do the homework and try to figure out how I was going to afford a new set of gaskets and pay for the train to work again. But I was still on a high, I had a twin of my very own, and Robert was due home next week. That was something to look forward to. He had been away for nearly a year, and had been promoted to third engineer.

At the end of that week I left Charlie, thanking him for spending so much time showing me the different ways to scrape the bearings. Even the cross-head bearings were scraped differently from the main bearings, a small concave area in being left in the centre of the bearing. This was to allow for the pressure when the engine fired, spreading the load equally along the bearing. Harland and Wolff engines were famous worldwide, and renowned for their dependability and workmanship. In later years, I felt proud when I told other engineers that I had served my time at Harland's they never had a bad word to say about our engines be they main engines or generators.

I knew the reason why the engines were so dependable!

Chapter 22

ENGINE ASSEMBLY

My new journeyman was Harry Bruce. Harry was very experienced in engine assembly and taught me an awful lot in the few weeks I was with him. (Robert was to marry Harry's wife's sister Valerie, a few years later.) There were bits of engines lying everywhere, but Harry had a plan of the lay-down areas and knew exactly where every piece was located.

He took me round the different assembly areas again, some of which I had already worked in and some that I had passed by with interest. The first area was the scavenge pump assembly area. Large two-stroke diesel engines made at Harland's had inlet ports on the cylinder liners to supply combustion air. Once the engine was up to speed, turbo blowers supplied this air. However for manoeuvring and at slow speeds, the combustion air is supplied by a pump – the scavenge pump. This is bolted onto the end of the engine and is chain driven from the crankshaft.

We moved on to the bedplate area where the main bearings were being set up, and then onto the crankcase doors. These were massive steel doors fitted with explosion relief valves.

'If there is a build-up of oil mist due to heat inside the crankcase due to a bearing running hot, a crankcase explosion can occur,' explained Harry, as we stood for a minute watching the men test the relief mechanism springs. 'The explosion relief valves are fitted to the crank-case doors so that if there is an internal explosion, the relief valve operates and the pressure inside is relieved. If this didn't work, the pressure from the explosion would blow the door of its hinges. This happened to the *Reina Del Pacifico*; she was on sea-trials in Belfast Lough after an overhaul in at Harland's. She suffered a bad crankcase explosion and a number of our engine fitters and an apprentice were killed,' he finished.

I followed him round to our engine, which looked about half finished. I thought of all the departments that I had been in since leaving the training school, and reckoned that the engine room of a ship was a dangerous place to work and I made a mental note to write down all the possible dangers from fire or explosion I would encounter, and do my best to prevent them.

Although I would see the engine nearly finished, I would be away outside working when she was fired up for the first time. I helped Harry and his fitter's mate guide a piston into the last cylinder. This was carried out by clamping the piston rings and guiding the piston through a tapered entering sleeve, set on top of the cylinder, removing the clamp on each ring, just before it entered the sleeve. The piston was hung from the overhead crane and great skill was required in this operation.

I went into the scavenge space and guided the piston rod through the rod-gland and then Harry guided it into the crosshead bearing, securing it with the nut. I had also found out what the ring of holes round the liner was for that had been bugging me since I was in the piston ring department. These holes were threaded internally and quills were screwed into them. The cylinders were lubricated by the oil being pumped through these quills from the lubricators, via tiny copper pipes.

Robert arrived home in the middle of the week and brought me another fishing rod, this time from Singapore. It was made from tubular cane and was a whopper! He also brought me my first "spinning reel" which had a fixed spool and was made from bakelite.

'So this is your latest bike William, she is a buet. Can I have a go on her?' asked Robert.

We were out in the shed after tea and he was sitting astride my T bird.

'Sure thing, but take it easy, she is throwing oil out of every gasket,' I replied as he kicked her into life. He was away about ten minutes and came back up the path with the tears streaming out of his eyes.

'Boy I enjoyed that, but look at the state of my jeans, the bottoms look as if I dipped them in oil,' he laughed.

'I got her a few weeks ago, but I am saving up for a set of gaskets. They cost a fortune and there's no sense in buying just one or two at a time. I want to renew the whole lot at once then she will be sound,' I finished.

We went back into the kitchen and Mags was finishing off the tea dishes with Beth.

'Did you enjoy your tea Darky?' asked Mags. (She always called Robert Darky as he used to come home black from Mackies; a spinning mill manufacturer, where he had served his time.)

'Yes Maggie, (again he was the only one who got away with calling her Maggie) it was good to get some home cooked grub again. I had alligator steaks in Australia, snails in France and snake suppers in South America, but Ma's stew beats them all hands down. How much is a set of gaskets for the bike William?'

'About twelve or fifteen quid, depending where I get them from,' I replied.

'I'll go into Bangor tomorrow morning and see if I can get them any cheaper for you from the garage.'

Robert used to work in a local garage, before going to sea and he still kept in touch with his old mates there. In fact he had worked for them for a few weeks on his last leave, whilst waiting for his next ship, to give them a pull-out he boasted afterwards.

The next day at work I was telling Harry about Robert being home and about my ambition to go to sea as we bolted on a cylinder head.

'I go out on trials a lot Billy,' said Harry, 'and enjoy working and watch-keeping in the engine room, but I like coming home after a few days. I don't think I could stick being away for a year or so at a time.'

'It wouldn't bother me at all,' I replied. 'I am really looking forward to it, another couple of years to go and I am off, like a blur!'

We finished the head and started fitting the valves. The exhaust valve was a separate unit and bolted into an opening in the head. This was known as a poppet valve and was opened by a pushrod operated from the camshaft, driven of the engine. We set the gap at 20 thou, and tightened the lock-nut.

'When the engine is running, a good tip to remember is to watch the pushrod and make sure it rotates a bit when opening and closing the exhaust valve, this shows that there is sufficient clearance at the tappets. If it just sits there, it could mean that there is not enough clearance, leading to a leaking valve,' finished Harry.

Over the next couple of days we fitted the rest of the cylinder head valves; one air start, one relief and the three fuel valves per head and connected up the relevant piping runs.

On Saturday morning I went with Robert to the garage and we stood talking to one of the mechanics, called Piggy.

'Right Piggy, we need a good price for a set of gaskets for William's Thunderbird. Remember he is only an apprentice, like you and I used to be, so you know what it is like being friggin skint!' he said to Piggy.

'Give me a minute and I will phone a company that supplies our car engine gaskets, they should be the cheapest around here.'

We walked around the garage workshop, Robert pointing out his old bench and vice; his initials still welded to the vice. I was telling him all about working on the Harland's engines and he was very interested as he had never seen one as Bibby Line ships usually had Doxford engines as their main units. He told me he had seen an electrically driven ship. This had steam turbines, which drove generators and, the electricity produced drove the propeller shaft.

'Eight pounds, nineteen and sixpence is the best price I can get, said Piggy, 'but he gave me another thirty bob off as I told him they were for me. The full gasket set will be here on Monday afternoon.'

'That's dead on,' replied Robert. 'I will pay you now, seven quid okay Piggy?'

'Aye go on then seeing it's for a good cause,' replied Piggy, winking over at me.

We went into the Castle Arms pub for a pint on the way home and it turned into a bit of a session. I barely remember going home, luckily Ma and Da were away at my Aunt Flora's for the day, so I sneaked in and went up to bed and went out like a light.

'Good day yesterday boy,' said Robert, 'you can hold a few pints, for a nipper! Come on out to the shed and I'll give you a hand to clean-up the bike and get it ready for the new gaskets.'

We worked away together, cleaning all the oil of the frame and back tyre. Robert was telling me about the navy, Japan, Singapore, and the rest when Da appeared.

'I am off to Granny's; I'll see youse at dinner time. Make sure you clean all this oil off the shed floor William, that bundle of scrap of yours leaks oil like a sieve! I got it on my new wheels yesterday,' ordered Da, as he took off up the back lane on his new Honda 50.

This was a wee cracker of a bike. It had a 50cc four stroke engine, three gears and an automatic clutch. I had picked it up for him from the local dealers, a few weeks ago as he wasn't quite used to the foot-change gears, and I was very impressed with its performance.

'Tell you what William, I will pay for the gaskets and put them in, if I can have the bike for a few weeks whilst I am on leave, I fancy doing a bit of touring before I rejoin the ship in Liverpool.'

'Dead on!' I replied, 'but you don't have to pay for the parts, you can have the bike while you are on leave anyhow.'

'No, a deal's a deal, like I said I will treat you to the spares,' he replied.

So that's how I got the new gaskets fitted. Robert overhauled the T bird fitting the new gaskets, then went away for a week touring the south of Ireland. I worked out my last week with Harry in the engine assembly department.

Harry took me round to the drive end of the engine and showed me the dynamometer which Adie Smalkis, a Latvian was setting up.

'Adie sets the dynamometer to the calculated thrust of the engine and then we can check the output and check the engine, under different loads,' said Harry as we watched the man couple it up. 'Pity you won't see her firing up, but come on and I will show you the different coolers and pumps. This will be the same set-up on most of the engine-rooms, you will be working on at sea.'

We started off at the lube-oil system tracing the lines from the pump to the engine and back to the coolers, part of a bank of coolers, which were cooled by sea-water. Next was the starting air system and again, Harry pointed out the danger of explosion, if the exhaust gas leaked back into the air lines. We finished up at the turbo-blowers, which were connected to the main exhaust before going through the roof of the shop.

'At sea the exhaust gas goes through the turbo-blowers then through a wee boiler before it goes up the flue. This heats the water and produces steam and hot water for the accommodation,' said Harry, pointing to where the massive exhaust ducting met the roof.

Soon it was time to say cheerio to the engine-works, and head off to the outfitting and slips departments. I went to all my old journeymen on the Friday and thanked them for putting up with me for three years!

'Come back and see us when you have your chief's tickets Billy,' said Willie Ross, looking across to Bertie.

'I will do that, don't fear, you haven't seen the last of me!' I replied just as Big Eddie strolled over to us.

'Well boy, we're getting shot of you at last. Thank the Lord! Never thought I would see the day,' he said with what I could swear was a shadow of a smile. 'I better warn my mate in outfitting that you are coming. He will keep his eye on you! All the best boy, you have done we… ahem, not bad – good luck.' As near a compliment I would get from the big man.

Chapter 23

OUTFITTING – IN THE DEEP WATER

I was shifted outside to work in outfitting as I had finished my allocated time in the engine works, and would not be coming back. I still had to do a spell in outfitting, the dry-dock squad, and some time on the slips, to finish my training. The usual time in outfitting was six months, and I was really looking forward to this part of my apprenticeship.

I met the head foreman, another massive man with a red face, long sideburns and a moustache. He wore the usual green dustcoat and black bowler.

'Right boy, I will take you into the stores; your journeyman's bench is in a part of the stores. Big Eddie phoned me on Friday and told me you were coming.'

He introduced me to my foreman, Andy Night, and to Johnny Patton, my new journeyman. Johnny was pretty old, about fifty or so, and going grey. He was a wee man, flat cap, and brown boiler suit over his shirt and tie. I had noticed that nearly all the 'old hands' wore a checked shirt and a tie under their boiler suits, as did the foremen, inspectors and rate-fixers.

'How are you Willie; this your first time outside? Don't worry, we aren't a bad lot and you will soon get used to the noise,' said Johnny, looking over to the ships tied alongside the fitting out berth.

'Yes Johnny, this is my first time outside the engine works, is it always as noisy as this?' I asked, over the din.

'Aye, it's the caulkers and steel bashers, never happy unless they are making a racket. You should have heard it when we had riveters joining in the chorus as well!'

I looked round the workshop. One side was fenced off and used as stores. The other side was made up of three benches with vices, a drilling machine and a lathe.

It had a concrete floor and a wee man was pushing a brush over the floor and tidying up as he went.

'That's Seagull,' said Johnny pointing to the sweeper upper. 'Don't leave your piece box lying around or he will eat your piece, paper and all. Never saw anyone who could eat so much. All he does is eat and shit! That's how he got his name,' he said laughing.

I am going to like it here I thought, not as organised looking as the engine works, and not a lot of gaffers looking down on you from overhead offices either!

'Sit down on the bench a minute Willie and I will go over a few things with you,' said Johnny. 'Our job over the next few weeks will be working on the double bottom pipe work. The double bottoms are like another small compartment, between the bottom deck and the ship's shell. They are pretty small, but you will be able to crawl through them all right. The main thing to look out for is anyone cutting, burning or welding above you, while you are working.'

'On the main deck, always keep your eye out for the cranes. They are lifting some heavy loads over our heads all the time; there is normally a banksman who will bawl at you to get out of the way. There is talk of us having to wear hard hats soon; some of the other yards in England have started making their men wear them. We have to have a union meeting about it. You can come along but keep quiet,' he finished.

We went out of the workshop and crossed the roadway to the ships, which were tied up behind each other. We passed a massive Shell tanker, with its phosphor bronze propeller well out of the water; it must have been about twenty feet across the blades, which gleamed dully.

'That's the *Methane Progress* – first of Shell's liquid gas tankers, wouldn't fancy being aboard that one when it is loaded with gas – a floating bomb if you ask me,' said Johnny as we stopped at a cargo ship's gangway. (I was to work on her for a spell when Johnny was off ill and she was cavernous, she is shown on the slips on the front cover.) 'This is our baby, the *Weybank* – a bankline ship of Andrew Weir; one of our best customers . We built stacks of these – she is almost finished. We have about a week's work in the double bottoms, then the emergency fire pump in the fo'c'sle and the lifeboats to fit and test.'

'Are the engines fitted yet,' I asked.

'Yes, about a month ago; remind me to ask Sammy to tell you about them at lunchtime. He is an engine fitter,' he replied as we walked up the sloping gangway. This gangway ran from the jetty to the top deck, and another one ran from the jetty to a hatchway about halfway up the ship's side. The both had wheels at the bottom, which let it rise and fall with the tide. They had hessian sacking and batons nailed to them to prevent the men slipping on the wood.

We eventually reached the top of the gangway and as I stepped onto the main deck the noise hit me like a sledgehammer.

'Give me the bag of tools and follow me down this ladder Willie,' shouted Johnny, over the din. 'Don't hold the ladder by the rungs, but grip the sides. If you hold on by the rungs, the man above you might stand on your fingers!'

I stepped gingerly over the hatch cover onto the first rung of the ladder and started down after Johnny. The noise vibrated through my hands and feet into my body, rattling my teeth as I gripped the outsides of the ladder for grim death. Eventually we reached the bottom, after transferring ladders at about three stages and I stood beside Johnny every bone in my body singing!

'We are on the bottom of the hatches now, follow me down to the double bottoms,' shouted Johnny as he jumped into another hatch.

I hastily scrawled an "X" on the hatchway (George, my mate had given me this tip as he had got lost down the hatches a couple of times) before stepping over the small coaming and into the hatchway. I found myself standing on the steel of the ship's bottom, the hatchway up to my waist. I dropped to my hunkers and then on my hands and knees, following Johnny's retreating boots into the semi-darkness of the double bottoms.

We were in a steel tunnel, and crawled through many cutouts in the stiffeners. Stopping at last Johnny plugged in our extension lead (called temporary light) and sitting with his back against the steel side proceeded to light a fag, offering me one.

'Thanks Johnny, where on earth are we?' I shouted over the din of the metal bashers hammers and chisels. The noise reminded me very much of running a stick along iron railings, magnified about ten million times!

'This is where I finished the pipelines on Friday. We are about halfway between the bridge and the fore peak tanks. These pipes supply and discharge the for'ard ballast and fresh water tanks,' he replied, 'I am going to show you how to cut a gasket from this roll of insertion rubber.'

I watched him cut the joint, from the roll that he must have stashed on Friday, by hammering the rubber against the steel pipe. This left a perfectly formed gasket, identical to the pipe-flange.

'Now you try it Billy,' he bawled, 'Cut the centre piece out first, that way you don't leave it in the gasket and form a blockage in the pipeline.'

How could you forget to cut the centre out, I thought as I knocked it out first, using the ball end of the hammer. I knocked out a couple of boltholes, putting spare bolts into the holes, before starting the rest, as Johnny had shown me. I carried on making the joints and got to the fifth or sixth one, thinking this was a piece of cake, when whack! Down came Johnny's cap on my lughole. Boy that hurt you ould bugger, I thought!

'Centre part first Billy! This is most important. Keep your mind on the job and try to remember this boy! Now, start connecting the pipes together using your gaskets and bolts. Tighten one bolt first, then a bolt opposite and so on. You get an even pressure all over the two flanges, that way they will never leak.'

We carried on for what seemed like hours, the din never falling below less than a million decibels, the vibration still coursing through my bones and rattling my teeth.

'Away up and see Seagull and ask him for my tea, I am as dry as a bone shouting at you!'

I turned round, which was a feat in itself as the soles of my boots hit one side and my bowed head the other, which short circuited the vibration to my teeth, increasing it ten fold, and started back the way I had come. At last I saw daylight ahead, it really was like being in a tunnel. Reaching the hatch I climbed out and looked up to the top deck. It was miles away!

I started climbing and had only gone about ten or fifteen rungs up when I had my fingers stood on.

'Get you bloody hands off the rungs boy. Keep them on the outsides and look up when you are climbing!' shouted an irate caulker with an air chisel on a length of hose over his shoulder. 'Go back to the bottom and don't start climbing till the ladder is clear in future.' I beat a hasty retreat to the bottom, waiting for another bollocking as he stepped onto the deck beside me but he just glared at me, shook his head and sauntered off, the hose and chisel swinging like a snake from his shoulder.

I eventually made it to the top, stopping a couple of times at staging to let other men pass, as it looked like the ones coming down had the right of way. Boy it was nice to get a breath of fresh air and as I stood looking round me a voice from behind made me jump a mile

'And what do you think you are doing, a spot of sightseeing in Royal Avenue? Scott isn't it? No wonder Eddie Schoffield was pleased to get rid of you boy!' spat our head foreman, his face about an inch from my nose.

'Err. Yes, I mean no! I was just having a blow after climbing the ladders from the double bottoms,' I stammered.

'Are youse nearly finished down there, if you take much longer you will be out of your time, especially if you spend so much time gawping about up here! Where are you going anyhow?' he asked suspiciously.

'J-just to get some more bolts for the pipelines, we have run out,' I managed to stutter.

'Hurry up then, or that ould bugger Johnny will be asleep by the time you get back,' he replied, putting one foot on the handrails beside the top of the gangway and glaring at all in sundry about him.

I made it to the workshop without further mishap and staggered through the door, noticing Seagull glancing up from behind our bench. Walking over I discovered him boiling Johnny's can using an oxy/acetylene torch and doing a fine job of it.

'Right Nipper, take this up to Johnny,' he said, putting the steaming can into a sack, holding it hidden by the wire handle. 'Carry it like this and you won't get burned. Watch out for the gaffers, they don't like us having ten' o'clock tea-breaks!'

Thus informed, I stepped out of the hut straight into the foreman.

'Hi Andy,' I shouted, 'nice day for it.'

'Aye for some maybe, what's in your sack?'

'Just a few bolts and a bit of rubber gasket material; can you tell me who has the right of way on the ladders leading to the holds?' I shouted again.

'I'm not deaf boy stop your shouting! In answer to your question, whoever is the biggest and meanest usually gets the right of way, whether they are coming up or going down. Just watch yourself at the five o'clock horn. You could get killed in the stampede. Do you know the head foreman is at the top of the gangway?' he said, dropping me a very broad wink before going inside and bawling at Seagull for "his tae"!

I spied the gaffer still standing at the top of the gangway and as I stepped of onto the deck he stood in front of me.

'That's a heavy looking sack boy, bolts you said, what took you so long?' he asked looking pointedly at the sack.

'Bumped into Andy and he put me right about a few queries I had about the ladders and that.'

'I am sure he did! Off you go then, don't keep that old bugger Johnny waiting any longer, he is a grumpy old baskit if he doesn't get his tea on time. I should know, I was his apprentice a few years ago!'

I made it down to the bottom deck in one piece, and crawled back through the double bottoms, holding Johnny's can in front of me, being careful not to scald my hand and more than it already was!

'Good lad Billy Boy, I am ready for this. Any problems?' he asked innocently.

'Well, first I bumped into Andy outside the workshop and he must think I am some sort of a imbecile, as I shouted him a few daft questions at the top of my voice, to let Seagull know he was outside the door. Then, if that wasn't bad enough, I was stopped at the top of the gangway by the head gaffer, what's his name, and he kept me talking till I thought my hand would melt with the steam from your can!'

'Ach sure them two are all right, Jacky the head foreman was my apprentice about twenty years ago and Andy and I worked together on the tools, before he was made up and we are all in the same Lodge, so there's no problem. They were just having you on – but don't take advantage of them, still keep the can under the sack like the rest of the boys do.'

Chapter 24

SAFETY GEAR

Later that week Robert went back to sea again. The night before he left he came out to the shed to bid me farewell.

'Thought I would find you here, is the Thunderbird to your liking?' he asked

'Aye, dead on; I saw a lovely AJS twin over at M & T garage and they will give me a good trade-in on the T-Bird. Are you ready for the off.'

'Tell them who you are; Johnny and I were in the BB with Sammy Melon and we both know George Thompson; that's where they got the name for their garage Mellon and Thompson – M & T.'

'I am away first thing tomorrow; joining the old *Warwickshire* in Lisbon, back to my opposed piston Doxford twins. I feel that they are my babies now, this will be my fifth trip on her – that's over four years all told!' he replied. 'I just popped in to say cheerio and thank you for a lend of the bike. I am away out tonight and will still be in the land of nod when you go to work tomorrow. Don't sign with any shipping lines until I come back, then I will have a look at the options. I should be back in about nine or ten months. All the best, stick at the college and learn as much as you can in the yard.' He punched me on the shoulder and stuck a pound note in my hand.

I'll miss him, but I will heed his advice, I thought as I polished the old Triumph bike, then kicking her into life I sped up the back path and away up the Belfast road for a burn!

Back at work next day we were standing in the fo'c'sle out of the rain, waiting for the fire pump and engine to be hoisted up from the jetty.

'I hate this place, always pissing it down,' said Seagull, spitting expertly towards the handrails.

'It's not that bad Seagull, we could be working outside,' replied Johnny, winking at me.

We had been issued with hard hats; grey for the tradesmen, white for managers, blue and white for head foremen and blue for foremen. The water ran off them right down your neck!

The crane banks-man signalled to Johnny and we went out onto the deck as the fire pump dropped out of the sky and landed gently on a wooden pallet.

'Give me a hand to pull this inside Billy, you too Seagull,' ordered Johnny as the slings were released. 'Thanks Nails,' he said to the banksman. 'That's "nail in the boot Bobby" he's the best hand there is at slinging. He gets his name from the way he walks'.

We pulled it into the fo'c'sle, Seagull and me pushing and Johnny guiding it from the front. It was about the size of Uncle Jimmy's boat engine and about as heavy! We were no sooner through when the banks-man whistled again and we trooped outside in time to grab the diesel engine and guide it onto another pallet. We repeated the exercise and then the rigger came in and set up chain blocks above the equipment supports. Right enough, Bobby had a pronounced limp in his left foot and walked as if he had a nail in the boot!

The rigger slung the pump and landed it expertly on the steel support welded a few inches of the deck, and I shuggled it along with Seagull until Johnny was satisfied with its position. He then marked out the hold-down boltholes and the rigger lifted it back to the deck.

We drilled the holes and mounted the pump back on the support and bolted it down.

'What do you reckon is the next job Billy?' asked Johnny.

'Do the same with the diesel engine driver?'

'Nope, we need to level the pump first, hand me the spirit level and a couple of fox wedges.'

Johnny put the level on the pump outlet flange and loosening of a couple of foot bolts knocked in a couple of the tiny steel wedges until he was satisfied the pump was level.

'Check that Billy – what do you think, is it level?'

I checked the spirit level and the bubble was dead centre. It was a very accurate level, graduated along the bubble window in very fine lines, so you could tell it was dead on. Johnny inserted brass shims, knocked out the wedges and handed them to me.

'Right Billy Boy, now you do it,' said Johnny, taking out the shims, just as the head foreman came into the fo'c'sle.

I loosened the bolts and knocked in the wedges, but as I knocked in the last one, I hit the level but managed to catch it before it hit the deck.

'I don't know; these youngsters nowadays!' Then whack! Johnny's hat bounced of my head, much to the amusement of all concerned.

'Don't let that ould git frighten you boy, he hit me often enough when I was his boy,' although we wore flat caps then said Jacky. 'Let's see you try again – and take your time, this job can take six minutes or six hours!'

I started again and this time I was lucky, I had her levelled in about ten minutes put in the right amount of brass shims and got a round of applause. After lunch we did the same with the engine and then set up the drive coupling.

'This is the most important bit of the job Billy, if the coupling isn't lined up correctly, she will shake herself to bits and bugger up the bearings. Always remember that when you are working on emergency equipment; men's lives are at stake – so get it right!' said Johnny, as he aligned the coupling using slip gauges and feeler gauges, until it was dead on.

'I'll away and book the Lloyds man for the morning,' said Andy rushing off. I tidied up the tools with Seagull, and helped the rigger retrieve his slings and chain blocks and tackle.

'Take heed of what Johnny tells you Nipper,' said the rigger, out of the other men's earshot. 'He is the best there is, he'll be missed.'

'Why's that?'

'He is retiring soon, didn't anyone tell you? He is sixty-five, but is staying on to finish this ship before he goes,' answered the rigger.

The next day we waited for Mr Bailey, the Lloyds Surveyor to arrive.

'He'll not come till after tea, away and get my tea Billy, Seagull will have it ready,' ordered Johnny. I saw him in a different light today; he must have trained hundreds of apprentices over the years. He really was an excellent tradesman – if only he wouldn't hit me with his hat, I thought as I mounted the gangway with his tea, still using the sack method!

'This will be your new boy then Johnny; what's this one like, will you be chucking him over the side like the last one?' asked the Lloyds man, winking at me.

'Aye, you know yourself John, head full of mad dog's shit and knows it all,' answered Johnny, much to Seagull and Andy's amusement.

'It would make a change from getting belted with his hat!' I said laughing.

'Never did me any harm,' replied Mr Bailey!'

'Were you with him as well?'

'Aye Billy, before I went to sea with Blue Star line. I got my Chief's Tickets with them, before settling down and getting married. Now let's have a look at this pump, not that I need to check this "old hand's" work, I would stake my reputation on his word.'

This was a fitting tribute to Johnny and one that I remembered for a long time.

The lifeboats were next on the list, but we got waylaid to the bridge. When we got there Johnny was quite breathless, as it was a bit of a climb.

'Away and get me a can of tea Billy! I know it is only nine o'clock, but I am fair tuckered out today. I can't face going out on that staging. Tell Andy to send up one of the other fitters.'

'Don't be daft; I can go out on the staging. I don't mind heights,' I said crossing my fingers and toes!

After he had a cup of tea, Johnny's colour returned and he told me what needed to be done.

'This is the clear-view screen Billy that the captain and the officers on watch need to use. When it is pissing rain or there is a gale blowing, you can't see out of the bridge windows (they call them ports on ships, for some insane reason!) so they use this revolving screen.'

The screen was like a wee fan about a foot in diameter and rotated at great speed and in doing so enabled the watchkeeper to see through the rain or spray. It was at present hanging in bits and my job was to go out on the staging and bolt the mounting plate and gasket to the bridge window!

I stepped out onto the staging from the bridge wing, holding on for grim death. Johnny was yarning away to a carpenter crony, paying no attention to me. I looked down to the deck and grabbed onto the perimeter ropes of the staging and banged on the window to get Johnny's attention. I squared up the gasket and started inserting the small brass screws through mounting plate and then Johnny put the nuts on the other end and tightened them up.

I was almost finished, in fact on the last screw when disaster struck. I dropped the screw and following its progress to the deck, saw it bounce and disappear into a rubbish pile. Clambering back inside, I told Johnny and retreated, under the blows of his hat, back to the bridge wing and down the ladders to the deck. I looked for ages, on my hands and knees, until I came up against a pair of shiny boots, creased trousers and green coat!

144

'Say one for me while you are down there boy. What are you up to now?'

Looking up my heart nearly stopped, the head gaffer was staring at me, the usual stern expression on his face.

'I dropped a brass screw and Johnny sent me down to look for it. I was working out on the staging at the time.'

'Away to the stores and get another handful, there are thousands of them. The sparkies use them all the time. Johnny is just having you on, but be more careful in future!' he finished as he wandered off in search of some other poor unfortunate.

I made it back to the bridge and took a can of tea for Johnny as a peace offering. We finished the job and the sparkie hooked it up and gave it a spin.

'Dead on Johnny,' said the sparkie, 'the nipper got it centred right enough it's humming like a wee bee.'

'Should hope so, used up half the bloody screws in the stores in the process,' quipped my old hand!

I worked on all sorts of jobs with Johnny, we seemed to get all the futtery and safety jobs. I never let him carry anything, or climb out onto staging. The hard hats we had to wear were a pain in the backside! I never once hit my head on scaffolds, bulkhead doors, staging, ladders or anything else – until I wore the hat. Then everything jumped down and hit me on the head! I can tell you, it was well scratched within a few months and of course I had the Triumph emblem painted on the back! Still they had the advantage that you could spot the gaffers a mile away.

We had finished testing the lifeboats. This was done by loading the boats with sandbags to twice their normal weight and lowering them, testing the winch brakes in the process. I was setting the limit switches, along with our sparkie Maurice, he was a good lad and handy to have in our squad.

'Knock off the power to the switches Mo, and I will re-set them.' I said to Maurice. I had been at this for about an hour or so, but was taking my time with it as it had to be right. I was straddling the lifeboat, a foot on each side when the limit switch arm flipped out of its holder, and smacked me right between the eyes!

I was dead lucky on two counts; Johnny had made me wear a lifeline. This was worn over the shoulders and across the chest and attached by a clip to the winch. Also I had my hard hat on, the limit switch arm had hit the peak of my hard-hat first, taking a lot of the force from the return spring mechanism out of it. I still gave a few wobbles and was going over when Mo jumped onto the boat and grabbed me, laying me down flat on the bottom boards.

'My head is spinning Mo, where's Johnny?' I said almost crying, like a big baby.

'I am here my son, I am right beside you. Seagull's away for the First Aid man, never saw him go so fast in years. Take it easy now, don't try and sit up till they get back up here,' ordered Johnny, quickly taking control of the situation.

My head hurt like hell, and blood was running into my eyes, being wiped away by Johnny but I felt better as he re-assured me that the limit switch was in the bottom of the boat beside me.

'Must have been a faulty one Mo,' said Johnny, 'we'll take it back to the stores and kick up hell with them. Andy will phone the makers and bollock them as well!'

The First Aid man arrived with a stretcher and they loaded me on and took me to the Medical Centre, in the back of the gaffers van. It was a quick journey and soon I was sitting up drinking tea and having a few stitches inserted.

'Home for you boy,' ordered Jack, the gaffer, 'and no arguments, I will run you to the station.'

'But I have my bike with me,' I wailed, nearly crying again at the pain above my eyes.

'Aye well, give me the keys and Seagull will go to the sheds and bring it over to the workshop. We'll keep it in there till you are back at work. Don't worry about it, Seagull knows all about bikes.'

I was off work for a couple of weeks and still bear the scar to this day, nearly 50 years on! Seagull had cleaned up my bike and she was shining like a new pin when I got back.

'We had a bit of a whip-round for you Billy,' said Johnny, handing me an envelope.

'But I got my full pay while I was off,' I protested.

'Aye well, you had a hard knock and bore it like a man, so you are no longer to be referred to as the Nipper. Seagull will make my tea and yours and bring it to us on the ship! And it was my job to set up the limits on the boats, but if that had of happened to me I would have been a gonner; you're a good lad Billy.'

I stayed in the squad for the full six months, as Johnny wouldn't let me go with anyone else. Apart from the spell I had on the *Methane Progress* when he was off sick for a month where I worked on the deck at the winches and windlass, and the hatches for the skylights. These were operated by a set of chains and pulleys from a wee platform at the very top of the engine room to let the fresh air in and the heat out. It must get hot up here in the tropics, I mused. Little did I know!

When Johnny came back to work he gave me a few days with Sammy in the engine room. I was astonished at the compactness of the engines, pumps and boiler. It sure was a long way down from the top plates to the manoeuvring and control platform. He also let me go with the steering engine team of fitters and this was good crack. I marvelled at the hydraulic system and small bore pipework that ran from the wheelhouse right aft to the steering flat.

All too soon my six months were up and I bade a sad farewell to the outfitting squad. I gave them all a last wave as I started up the T Bird and took off up the deep-water jetty; ever mindful of the dreaded tram-lines. As I looked back, Johnny was waving his hard hat at me and pointing to his head! I knew what he was meaning all right – not the bump I got but the number of clips he gave me round the earhole!

Chapter 25

THE DRY-DOCK SQUAD

'Can you tell me where I can find Alex Curtiss please?' I asked a helper who was standing at the gangplank of a wee coaster.

'Aye, he's the engine squad gaffer, you will find him in the engine room.'

I looked down into the dock as I walked down the sloping gangplank between the dry-dock wall and the ship. It was a long way down and the coaster looked like a wee toy ship sitting on the bottom of the dock.

I made my way down into the engine room, avoiding all the usual pitfalls of hoses, ropes and tackle on the way. I saw a gaffer in a brown dustcoat and walked over to him.

'Excuse me,' I shouted over the usual din, 'I am looking for Alex Curtiss.'

'You've found him. Who are you?'

'Billy Scott, fourth year apprentice fitter. I was told to report to you this morning.'

'Where did you last work?'

'Outfitting with Johnny Clarke,' I replied.

'Is old Johnny still on the go, I thought he had retired years ago. How is the old bugger, still rattling you with his cap?'

'Aye, not so much now, thank goodness, as we wear the hard hats!' I answered laughing and tapping my lid.

'Right Billy, you go along with Colin in there,' he said, pointing to a young man who was working in the crankcase. 'Ever do any scraping or taking leads?'

'Yes, did a bit with Charlie Carson in the engine works. I was only there for a couple of months though.'

'Good, we can do with you in this squad, we are a couple of men down with this damn Asian flu bug!' he finished as we swung into the crankcase.

'This is Billy, Colin. Says he has done a bit of scraping in the engine works, so he should be able to help you out till the rest of the squad gets back, if they ever do!' He bawled, leaving me with Colin.

'Give us a hand out with this bearing cover Billy, put one foot inside the crankcase door and the other on the crank,' said Colin, swinging a bearing cover over to me. The helper was outside waiting to take it from me and the operation went well. Colin was fairly sweating, and had a cloth tied across his forehead.

'Sling your hat over there beside your bag, and come on inside,' he said to me signalling to the main bearing.

I climbed inside and sat on the bearing whilst Colin sat on the opposite one. I looked around the dimly lit crankcase. It was covered in oil, as you would expect. The piston rods and cranks were shining and reflecting the string of temporary lights that were hanging from various positions like Christmas tree lights.

'Away up to the stores on the jetty and ask the store man for a roll of lead wire Jimmy,' Colin said to the helper, 'and take a few clean rags down with you as well. See if Sammy-no-more has posted the overtime shifts yet.'

'Jimmy is as good as another fitter; he has been here longer than me. What year are you in Billy?' asked Colin.

'Fourth year, I hope to go to sea next year.'

'I was away for a few trips with Bank Line, but the wife got preggers and that put a stop to it. I enjoyed myself mind you. It is a great life for a single man.'

Jimmy arrived back and told Colin that there was overtime for two nights, Saturday morning and a Sunday.

'Want to work tomorrow night Billy? Jimmy and I could do with you; we have a lot on over the next week, and will be pushed to get all the work finished before they flood the dock. We need the genny's and main engines ready by then,' Colin asked.

'Sure, I will bring a big piece,' I replied.

We worked away all morning, removing the bearing tops and checking for wear and high-spots. Lunchtime came and Jimmy went off with the cans whilst Colin and I cleaned our hands and sat down on a couple of wooden boxes.

'We will take the leads after lunch and then you can run up to the gaffers office and get him to call in the Lloyds man for tomorrow morning,' said Colin, biting into a sandwich and slurping his tea from the can. Jimmy had made a grand can of tea and I was ready to go again just as the horn blew.

'I'll away up with the cans Colin, want anything while I am up there?' asked Jimmy.

'No, but hurry back as we need to take a set of leads from the bottom ends before we knock off,' answered Colin.

We worked away taking the leads, it was hard going as the bottom half of the bearing had to be lowered to the bottom of the sump, then lifted again and bolted up to check the clearance, on every cylinder. Not only that, but the piston rod had to be disconnected as well. She was a six cylinder Polar engine and we were doing a cylinder at a time, bottom ends and main bearings. Jimmy had done three cylinders by the time I came to work for him so we were half way there.

'Do we strip the gennys as well Colin?' I asked.

'Usually we do, but they got a squad in from the garage to overhaul them as we are so short of men in our squad,' he answered. 'Right Billy, go up to the office and tell the gaffer that we are ready for the Lloyds man in the morning. If he is not in his office, go to the one above and let Sammy-no-more know and he will organise it.'

I went up the stairs and onto the deck. It was teeming down cats and dogs as I ran across the gangway onto the jetty.

'Watch out boy! You nearly had me over the edge then,' said an irate voice. I looked up and brushed my wet hair away from my eyes.

'Sorry sir,' I replied to Mr Angry. He wore the white hat of a manager.

'Where are you off to in such a hurry? You will have to learn to walk when you are working in my squad, very dangerous to run you know!'

I was on my way to Alex Curtiss, to get him to order up the Lloyds man. If I couldn't find him I was to report to Mr No-more,' I replied.

'Don't know who that is, but I will let the Lloyds man know. I am Mr Agnew, your manager.'

'Pleased to meet you, I am Billy Scott and have just started today with Colin Graham, working on the main engine.'

'Right, I am on my way down to see how they are getting on; you follow me down boy!'

I followed him down and we stopped outside the crankcase.

'Are you there Colin?' he shouted into the crankcase.

'Aye, Oh it's yourself Mr Agnew, the boy found you then?'

'Bumped into me more like; I have told him not to run about on the deck or gangway. Very dangerous you know. Please keep an eye on your apprentice. He is your responsibility you know,' he finished and turned on his heel and walked away.

'Silly ould shit, that Agnew,' spat Colin. 'Jumped up snob, if ever there was one.'

'Who is this Sammy-no-more then?' I asked.

Both Colin and Jimmy nearly pissed themselves laughing.

'That's yer man,' they both said together, 'he used to be our head foreman; until he got made up to manager. He told us to call him Mr Agnew now that he was a manager and not to call him Sammy-no-more!' This was where he got his nickname!

I was at home later that night and Mags was making up the pieces.

'Make a few extra for me Mags, bread and jam will do. I am working till seven tomorrow and Thursday night.'

'No bother child. Don't be working too hard now; you are supposed to have a bit of fun, you know. Working two nights and two nights at tech takes up most of your week.'

'I know, but I am saving up for a new bike. I saw a super one last week and the guy said he would give me fifty quid for my old bike as deposit against the new one. I finished breathlessly.

'Ma and Da were away looking at a car earlier on. They went to bed before you came in from the tech. They seemed quite taken with a wee Morris Minor. You could maybe go with them tomorrow night after work and have a look at it with them.'

'Sure will. Didn't know Da was thinking about another car. Mind you I would still like to learn to drive if I get the chance,' I said as I headed up the stairs.

Da had traded in the Honda 50 for an old side valve Morris Minor a while ago and was always at me to learn to drive before I went off to sea.

'Night Mags, tell Da I will be in about half eight tomorrow night and I will go and see the new car with him if he'll wait till I get home.'

I got in about eight the following night and after downing my dinner, I left with Ma and Da to see the car. It was over in Flood's Service station on the Clandeboye Road, a short walk away and next door to the M & T garage where the AJS was for sale.

'There she is what you think of her William?' asked Da as we approached a turquoise Morris.

'She is a beaut, can we have a go in her?'

'Hang on and I will get the keys,' said Da disappearing into the garage. 'Jump in and we will go for a spin up the Rathgael Road.'

Ma got in the back and I got in the passenger seat.

'It's a wee bit out of our money range William, but Da is going to ask if we can pay it up,' whispered Ma, as if half of Bangor was listening to her taking on tick. Da got in and started her up.

We went to the top of Rathgael Road where he stopped and offered me a fag. 'What do you think of her? Doesn't she run well?'

'Sure does, but how much will it cost?' asked Ma.

'Well Sam Flood will take the old Morris as a full deposit and we pay twenty quid a month,' answered Da.

'Oh we couldn't afford it Francie,' cried Ma.

'I didn't think so but it would be a shame to miss such a bargain.'

'I will chip in a tenner a month.' I heard myself say.

'Are you sure son, it will be for a year you know, and then there's the tax and insurance as well.' Replied Da.

'Sure I'm sure, as long as you teach me to drive!' I shouted.

We signed the papers that very night and Da said he would pick her up at the weekend once he had the insurance sorted out. There was even three months road tax on her!

I went next door and signed up for HP on the AJS, noticing for the first time that she was first registered in 1959, and I was her second owner! I managed to wrangle £60 for the Triumph, after telling the salesman that she was just overhauled; and would pick up the AJS on Saturday, as they wanted to give her a check-over and service.

I was telling the boys at work the next day and they said we had both got good bargains; my Da had got nearly the full price back on his old car, and I doubled what I had paid for the T bird.

The Lloyds surveyor arrived and checked the bearings and leads, signing off another cylinder, which left us two to finish.

'Don't forget we have to pull the pistons and renew the rings after we finish in here,' said Colin.

'And take the crank deflections,' quipped Jimmy. 'Never mind; lots of overtime, the gaffer says we can work five nights and the weekend if we want!' Great I thought, just what I need right now, plenty of overtime to pay off the new bike.

We finished off the bearings at the weekend and Colin showed me how to take the crankshaft deflections. This was done to ensure that no undue stress was put on the cranks and bearings because of the ship's hull alignment. Colin used an inside

Me astride the 650cc AJS SS; my pride and joy; I worked long hours to get her.

micrometer, with about a foot extensions on each side of it! We took readings at top and bottom dead centres, then a couple of readings about halfway mark. These were compared with the original readings for the engine when it was new and shown to the Lloyds man.

'I seem to be following you around Billy Boy,' said the Lloyds man.

'Sure seems that way right enough Mr Bailey. Have you seen Johnny lately?' I asked him.

'Aye, saw him a few days ago; he is retiring this Twelfth Holidays, that's fifty years he has worked in the yard, not counting his six years in the Paras during the war.'

'I never knew he was in the Paras,' I gasped.

'Yes, well he doesn't talk about it much, with the troubles and that and him being shy like.'

'Shy! Johnny! Are we talking about the same man here? Sure he must have hit me about a hundred times with his hat,' I laughed, but I remembered how he had calmed me down when I had my accident and how he seemed to take control of the situation, the men obeying his commands without a second thought.

'How's this young-un coming on Colin?' he asked, pointing at me.

'Oh, he'll do, no afraid to get stuck in and likes his ovies as well, don't you Billy Boy?'

'Here we go again, Billy Boy, will I ever lose this name.'

'Nothing wrong with a name like that; at least we know what foot you kick with now, thanks to Mr Bailey! shouted Jimmy, as I swung a fist at him.

'Well, that's us finished the bottom ends for now, we will pull the pistons next week and we should be ready to fire up on schedule,' said Colin. 'I think we will have an early night tonight. My wife thinks I am back at sea again – I wish!'

'And I have a week's work to catch up at the Tech. It's the exams next month as well'' I said.

'Its City and Guilds you are sitting Billy, isn't it?'

'Yes Colin. I have finished and submitted the metalwork piece. We had to make a reamer for the first part and a go-no go gauge for the second part. I think I did okay; mind you the teacher helped me a lot on the new 'Cincinnati' miller. It's very complicated piece of machinery,' I replied.

'Yea, I know, my brother works in the engine works machine shop and they have had a couple of new ones installed. He had to go to Italy for a week's training on CNC mills. Lucky dog – Italian Senoritas!' he laughed.

I spent a couple of hours catching up on the essays I had to do for night school and went down to Toni's on the bike.

'Coffee please Toni, quiet tonight eh?' I said as I slid on to the seats at the counter.

'Your friend Derek was in earlier – with a girl! He said he would be back in after the pictures; he lika the James Bonda,' replied Toni.

Well I never, Derek with a bird, this I must see. I had been having a few of my own over the last year. I sat chatting about the bikes to a couple of mates and was just about to go home when Derek walked in with a cracker of a girl on his arm.

'What about you Willie? This is Rosie. Rosie, meet my mate Willie,' said Derek as I ordered them a drink.

'Pleased to meet you Rosie.'

'Likewise I'm sure,' she replied in a broad Belfast accent. 'That your old Thunderbird outside, bet it's not as fast as my Derek's Velo. He can handle her as well,' she finished giving me a knowing look.

'Well you are right about one thing, she is faster than mine,' I replied.

We cracked on about the bikes for a while and then Toni threw us out at half eleven.

'Fancy a burn Willie?' asked Derek, 'The roads should be quiet at this time of night.'

'No me, I'm for bed, I have been working seven days a week lately and am well and truly knackered.'

'Probably doesn't want to get blown off Derek,' said the mouthpiece on his arm.

'On the contrary, as Derek well knows, I am always up for a burn, but not tonight Josephine!'

I left them outside Toni's talking to the rest of the bikers; they were off to Belfast by the back roads. This was a favourite racetrack for us, especially at this time of night, but I was not in the mood.

Next day at work we started pulling the pistons, I was in the crankcase letting go the bottom ends and Colin and Jimmy worked the overhead crane. This was very hard going as we were up against the clock.

Once the piston was clear of the cylinder, I went topside to help remove the old rings. We used a clamp with an adjustable screw for this.

'Come on over to the cylinder Billy and I will show you how to "size" a cylinder liner, and check for wear,' said Colin, pointing to the gaping hole that the piston had left in the engine block.

'You take the internal mic and measure the diameter at four positions round the circumference at 3, 6, 9, and 12 o'clock. Then repeat this at halfway down the liner and finally at the bottom dead centre,' Colin instructed and I started writing down the readings as he shouted them out.

'Hold on a minute Colin,' I shouted, 'you are going too fast! Let me make a wee sketch first, then I will only have to jot the readings down.'

I made a rough sketch of the liner and marked in the locations that the readings were to be taken.

'Right, start again Colin, fast as you like now!' I shouted confidently just as Sammy-no more stopped beside me.

He never interrupted us, just stood beside me watching me writing down Colin's readings.

'Right Billy Boy, that's the lot for cylinder number one, give me a hand out of here, my legs are cramping,' Colin's voice echoed from inside the engine.

'Let me see the readings boy,' ordered Sammy-no-more.

He studied these in silence and handed them over to Colin.

'What do you think Colin?' he asked.

'The cylinder is within tolerances given to me by the chief engineer, but Lloyds will want to see these and probably witness a few others,' replied Colin. 'Nice sketch Billy Boy!' he said to me.

'Yes, I thought so too; we may get the drawing office to make copies of your sketch for use on other engines. Well done Billy,' said Sammy.

Well, praise indeed from a manager and all! And, he called me Billy!

We carried on working all that week twelve hours a day. I was truly knackered and missed another couple of night classes but managed to get a day off for day release. The exams were approaching and I really would have to get my skates on and start revising.

The dock was flooded on Monday, on schedule, the gaffers were right pleased and were down below with us as the gennies were started when the coolers had seawater supply and soon we were generating our own electricity and dropped the shore supply. The garage mechanics had done a good job on the gennies and the old Chief Engineer complimented them.

'The tug is alongside and ready to tow us out, so the engines are on "Standby" boys,' said the Chief, who was at the main controls. The engine-room was getting noisier as a couple of air compressors and all the pumps were now running, adding to the racket made by the two generators.

Clang, clang, clang, rang the bells of the engine room telegraph as the chief answered it and turned the engine over on air. Colin was up at the cylinder heads and he shut the indicator cocks as soon as the engine had turned over.

'All clear!' he shouted.

The chief gave the engine another blast of compressed air and then put the fuel lever over to run. This was like opening the throttle on the bike or pushing down the accelerator on a car. The engine fired up with a loud roar and the whole floor vibrated as the chief gave her big licks.

Clang, clang, clang, the telegraph rang again and this time it was for ahead. The chief stopped her and I saw the reversing gear operating and once it had inter-locked, he hit the compressed air again. Away she went, this time ahead with little or no vibration.

'How do you like this Billy?' asked Colin sidling up to me and stopping between the chief and me.

'Dead on, what was all the loud blasts and shouting about?'

'Oh, we leave the indicator cocks open to blow any shit or water out of the cylinders whilst she is turned over for the first time on air. Then the chief was waiting until I shouted that they were all shut before he fired her up in earnest!' he answered and the chief nodded.

'What's the third doing Colin?'

'He's taking the movements and the time they are requested on the bridge and engine-room telegraph, recording them in the movement book. You'll see a few of those books in your time at sea Billy,' he answered, nodding to the third engineer.

All too soon we got finished with engines rung on the telegraph. The third handed the movement book to the chief and he took off up the engine room steps two at a time.

'Fairly moves for his age, don't he?' asked the third.

'Sure does,' replied Colin, 'What's he like to sail with?'

'Dead on, we never see him down here unless we need him. That's the way we like it. The second engineer runs the show, he is Dutch, but he's all right as well. He's on leave still, he and the fourth are due back tonight and then we take bunkers and head off for Liverpool tomorrow night,' replied the third, whilst putting in the turning gear. 'Do you want to have a quick shuftie inside before you go back up Colin? I'll be opening the doors shortly for a final check once she cools down a bit.'

'No thanks! Seen enough of her in dock, come on Billy, we are out of here. All the best mate, hope the main engine behaves better for you after the overhaul. If it don't – blame Billy Boy, he did the major overhauls!' He shouted to the third and nodded to the donkey-man who had just joined us on the control platform.

We shook hands all round; I looked back enviously and waved to the men as I followed Colin up the engine room steps. The sweat was running off me. I noticed that the engineers wore little under their white boiler suits and had mentioned this to Colin. He said he used to wear only his ball-bags under the boiler suit, as it got very hot in the engine room.

'See you in the morning Billy,' shouted Colin as we parted at the time office.

'Dead on Colin; that was the best ever!' I answered and pulled on my skidlid.

'What's for dinner Ma? I am starved. Do you know I was in the engineroom today and we moved the ship out of dry-dock. I was standing right beside the chief engineer!' I shouted excitedly as I came in the back door.

'Slow down William, you are going to blow a gasket!' replied Da who was already at the table.

'I never realised I was late, sorry Ma but today just flew by,' I said as I sat down to a plate of stew.

After dinner I went up to my room to revise and was doing quite well until the room door opened and big Noel stuck his head round it.

'Got a few *Shooting Times* for you, remember you said you would lend me a couple of *Motor Cycle News* Mags?' he asked.

'They are on my dresser over there,' I pointed with my pen.

'Your Ma said to tell you to have a blow. There is tea in the pot in the kitchen.'

We went downstairs and into the kitchen and I poured a couple of cups of brew. Noel offered and lit the fags and we sat for a few minutes in companionable silence.

'I pick up my AJS on Saturday morning, can't wait to give her a good burn!'

'I am out of my time next week,' Noel replied out of the blue, 'that's me a fully trained plasterer!'

'Good for you, how's the new building site coming on?'

'Pretty good, we are on piece rate and making a bomb at it! I had thirty five quid top line last week!'

'No kidding, that's more than my Da makes and he is a ganger!'

'Aye, but he gets a good rate every week, we just get that on piece work,' he replied, finishing his tea.

'I will have four years done in September and when Robert comes home in October, he is coming to the Board of Trade Offices in Belfast with me. If I pass my exams and get a grading I could be at sea before Christmas!'

'When's your exam?'

'Next week,' I replied, as I glanced guiltily at the kitchen clock.

'Better let you get back at it then,' he said as he went towards the back door, tucking the magazines under his arms. 'The mackerel should be in soon, your exams will be over by then, surely,' he said. I don't think he rated exams very highly.

'Hope so, but I'll be working two nights and the weekends after the exams, if these past months are anything to go by,' I replied.

'See you at the weekend anyhow, cheerio! he said as he closed the back door.

Before I knew it the exams were on me. Today, Wednesday I had Maths in the morning and Mechanical Drawing in the afternoon. Tomorrow was Mechanics in the morning and Strength of Materials in the afternoon. I had already completed the metalwork project and Mr Peden thought I would do okay in it, so I would pass at least one subject, I thought.

The maths wasn't too bad; I avoided one calculus question, and had a stab at the other. The rest was multiple choice; algebra, trig and geometry.

'How did you get on Willie?' asked one of the lads as I joined them in the shelters for a fag.

'Not bad, I think. I did all the questions but probably fluked the calculus and geometry ones. Still I think I did enough to pass,' I replied, taking out a piece from my lunch tin.

'That's seen better days Willie,' said Garry, a mate from Donaghadee. He worked in Mackies Spinning Mill.

'I'll have you know this lunch-box is nearly four years old and has seen most areas of the yard!' I replied.

I turned over the techie drawing question paper with trepidation. This was a two-hour paper and I knew I would be knackered at the end of it, as I had to stand stooped over a drawing board for that amount of time. One of the exam questions was to draw a marine diesel engine fuel valve or a safety valve in front and side elevations, with a section through it showing the internals. I was in luck and chose the safety valve as it was less complicated of the two choices. I worked out the best scale and got stuck in.

The classroom was very quiet as we were all beavering away;

'Youse have half an hour left,' shouted the "Leaper" and we all nearly jumped out of our skins. I had completed the section and just had to make the notes and list the parts. I finished just as the leaper called time and sat down completely drained.

'What's up Scott, drawing too hard for you?' asked the Leaper sarcastically.

I nearly told him where to go but stopped short, remembering that I had only one more day to go and I was finished with school for good! I gathered up my pencils and rubber, grabbed my bag and headed for the door. Donning my skidlid I leaped onto the T-bird and let her rip! I headed for the open road for a good burn and was just touching the ton when I saw a car pulling out about a hundred yards away. There was no way I was going to be able to overtake it, as there was a big 'Charles Neill' coal lorry coming the other was. I slowed down a bit but was still doing over eighty and took a chance, slipping up the inside of the old banger between it and the grass verge. As the grass whipped against my socks, I looked into the car and the old dear in the passenger seat nearly lost her false teeth as I flashed by! Clearly neither of them had seen me coming. I stopped up the road and waited for the old eejit to stop beside me.

'You nearly killed me then you old fool,' I shouted as he wound down his window.

'You were going too fast, this is a forty mile an hour speed limit you know!' he answered, the old dear whittling on beside him.

'Oh bugger off you old eejit, look right the next time before you come out onto a main road! And get her a pair of falsers that fit, she nearly swallowed that pair!' and at that I kicked the T bird into first and roared off, leaving them in my smoke and dust stream.

I was still in a mood when I got back to the house.

'How did the exams go?' asked Ma innocently as she stirred the soup.

'Don't ask!' I answered and stormed up the stairs to my room. I opened the wardrobe door and took out all the schoolbooks that I had used over the last four years and put them all into a big "Kellogg's" cardboard box. I tied the box closed with a piece of catgut and put the whole lot up in the attic.

I lay down on the top of my bed then sat up shaking like a leaf. I rushed through to the bathroom and was sick about five times, finishing with a final long dry boke!

'Everything all right son?' asked Ma through the bathroom door.

'Aye dead on now, I was just a wee bit sick,' I answered.

'Must have been nerves after your exams finished.'

Aye, I thought, if only you knew Ma, you nearly got a visit from the cops, picturing again the whole scene of the car coming out in front of me.

I brought all the exam papers into work as Sammy-no-more wanted to see them.

'How did you get on?' he asked

'Okay, I think, the maths was a bit of a stinker but the rest was much as the teacher told us it would be. I could have done with a bit more time for revision, but I appreciate the time off that you gave me.

'Well, I shall expect a lot of work out of you now; you have only a few months left here. I can tell you now that you are to be shifted to the garage next and then your last six months will be on the slips. I recommended you for a spell in the garage after the good job you did on the last ship's engines,' he finished.

Praise indeed, I thought. Colin came into the office and asked about the next job. He had been made up to foreman as Alex had retired early due to his ulcers and piles. He worried too much and was always dashing about, but I would miss him as he was good crack!

'We have a tanker coming in for three months, full overhaul of engines, generators and boilers. I will give you a list what Lloyds want to witness. I was just going over Billy's next moves with him,' Sammy said to Colin.

'We could do with keeping him with us for another six months. Could you ask the Apprentice manager Sammy?' replied Colin.

'I suppose so; we are due another couple of tradesmen and a new apprentice as well. I will see what I can do. How do you feel about that Billy?'

'Suits me fine,' I replied, 'but remember I want to go to sea as soon as I am out of my fourth year. That's only four months away.'

'We'll cross that bridge when we come to it. I have the final say in that,' replied Sammy-no-more.

Come Saturday I had the day off, so went and picked up the AJS, big Cecil was with me as I handed over the T Bird log book and keys. I kicked the big twin into life and took her for a spin to see if she was ok after the service.

I drew up back at the garage and Cecil saw the look on my face

'What's up William?' he asked.

'Only does 70 flat out now; she nearly did the ton when I tried he before they serviced her,' I replied.

'Lets have a look and see what they have done; you tube – you had the choke lever right across to full choke. No wonder she was going slow, you were choking her to death!' said Cecil, the salesman looked on rather bemused at my red face. I had no idea there was a choke lever on the handlebars – the other bikes I had previously owned had the choke at the carburettor air inlet.

Chapter 26

BOARD OF TRADE GRADING

Robert had been home a few days and I finally got a chance to speak to him up in our room.

'I can get a day off this week and we could go to the Board of Trade office in Belfast to see if they will grade me,' I opened.

'Okay, if you are sure that's what you want, I will phone them tomorrow and get you an interview,' he replied.

Good as his word, as soon as we were alone the next night Robert told me we were on for Friday.

'They will get in touch with the yard manager, and you will need to take a copy of your exam certificates,' said Robert.

'I don't mind that, I'll tell them to phone Sammy Agnew for a reference, and they can write to the Apprentice Training Manager, for a copy of my indentures.'

We got the train to Belfast on Friday. Ma and Da knew what we were going to town for and hadn't said too much, Da at least understood as he had been at sea for years and knew how I longed for the sea. We were told to wait in an old fashioned room, all oak panelled and paintings of old naval ships.

'Mr Scott? Would you come this way please,' asked a mousy looking women with wire specks on her nose. She showed me into a room where three men in suits sat behind a long desk and one of them showed me a seat in front of the desk and told me to sit down.

'Tell me a bit about yourself and why you want to go to sea as an engineer,' invited the middleman.

'Well, I am twenty years old next month and I will have four years of my time served as a marine fitter.'

'Where are you serving your time?' asked left man.

'Harland and Wolff.'

'Carry on.'

'I have wanted to go to sea since I was a wee boy. My granddad and my father were on the fishing boats and my brother is an engineer with Bibby line. I hope to go when I have completed four years, if you give me a grading.'

'What qualifications have you?' this from Mr Right hand.

'I passed across my City and Guilds Certificate and Junior Tech Certificates.'

'Good, now we are going to ask you a few questions about engines, so don't look so worried lad, we only want general answers to get an idea how much you have learnt so far.'

'How would you re-pack a stern gland?

'Remove the old packing with a tool like a corkscrew and then give the shaft a rub with emery and grease it. Cut the packing to size and mitre the ends. Stagger the joints around the gland and knock each packing ring home with a dog-leg stick.'

'Why do you scrape bearings and how do you check the oil clearance?'

I answered this and about five or six more, along with a couple of questions on safety and they seemed impressed when I told them how I was trained to assemble and test air-start and relief valves.

They sat huddled together for about a minute then Mr Left cleared his throat.

'Well boy, you have been fortunate to have had a very good grounding in engineering. This will certainly stand you in good stead in your future career as an engineer. I have to check with Mr Cummings and Mr Agnew, but I am sure there will be no problems. I can tell you now that on production of your indentures, we can certify you as Grade A, for purposes of seagoing engineer. Well done lad!'

I couldn't believe it; I shook hands with them all and walked out of the room on air!

'Grade A Robert!' I shouted as the door closed behind me.

'Dead on, let's go to the Pool and see if there are any vacancies for Junior Engineers, but first we'll go for a pint to celebrate.'

We walked into the "Crow's Nest" to be greeted with shouts from a couple of Robert's mates who set a couple of pints up in front of us.

'This young-un has just been been granted a Grade A! What about that. I was a Grade C, and I had done five years of my time,' boasted Robert.

We had another couple of pints and the two other lads insisted coming to the

Pool with us – for moral support and to give advice, although they were well away with the old Guinness.

We walked into the Pool. It was a large building crowded with men and clouds of smoke swirling from a million cigarettes and pipes.

'Over here William, that's for the catering and AB's departments. This is for the Ship's Engineer Officers.

'Here's a Bank boat needing a junior, away up and ask what the rate is William,' said Matty, one of Robert's mates.

'What's the rate for Junior's on the Bank line ship?' I asked a man behind the counter.

'Sixty quid a month, want to get in touch with them?'

'No thanks, just asking.'

'Trident Tankers look good, if you like oil tankers. I was with Shell and BP for a few trips, good money,' said Bobby, the other half Robert's team.

'What's the rate for Junior's with Trident Tankers?' I asked the same wee man.

'What's your grade son?'

'Grade A, in a few weeks time, so I am really just looking, with my brother and his mates, I pointed over to the boys, who were examining the boards with interest.'

'Good; 86 – 100 quid a month, if you sign six-month articles; come back with your Board of Trade grading in writing son, and I guarantee I will get you a ship and have you away within the week,' he answered.

'Thanks, I will see you then.'

We all walked back across the Queen's Bridge and into the railway station bar. After another couple of pints we left the boys and Robert and I boarded the Bangor train.

'What a day! I still can't believe it,' I said as the train pulled out of the station.

'Got this off Matty for you,' said Robert.

It was a Merchant Navy book, with bags of companies advertising for seagoing engineers. My next job was to get application forms filled in for my seaman's discharge book and card. Robert had got me these while I was being interviewed.

'Got a call from an old mate of mine yesterday asking all sorts of questions about you boy,' said Sammy-no-more the next morning. 'Give you a clean bill of health, I did and he was mighty impressed with you as well, still he's easy pleased,' he finished winking at Colin. I had a word with the Apprentice Manager as well, so you should have no bother getting your grade next month.

Chapter 27

AWAY TO SEA!

A month later to the day, I received a brown buff envelope with the Board of Trade and HMS insignia stamped on it. Opening it up I took out a slip of paper which certified me as having passed the BOT interview and been graded Grade A. This was what it was all about, I thought. I looked across to where Ma and Da were sitting and blinked back the tears.

'I got it!' I said, 'At last!'

I had written to several companies and almost decided on Trident Tankers. They were a subsidiary of P & O Liners and paid top dollar for engineers. I sent off for my seaman's book and card, along with a copy of my grading and a few weeks later I received them. I had already got my passport.

I was all set. I had given my notice into the yard and Friday was my last shift, as I had a couple of weeks holidays to take and intended to use this time to get my uniform together.

I heard back from Trident Tankers nearly right away, offering me a post of Junior Engineer and putting me on pay, from my last shift at the yard. Robert donated his old uniform and I bought my whites and Far East gear from the Merchant Navy Outfitters in Belfast.

Trident Tankers lost no time, I received the gold braid and cap badge the next day along with a list of gear as long as your arm, including a cummerbund, which had us all fooled, but Sergeant Rankin, Da's friend in the RUC put us right. It was a black band of silk worn round your waist, when dressed for dinner in shirt and slacks.

I had finished my last shift at the yard and had arranged to meet the boys in the "Crow's Nest" pub at seven. I rushed round the table and headed for the train station – no bike for me tonight. I thought of selling her, but couldn't bear the thought of parting with her; so my Da said he would give her a turn over and Robert would use her when he was on leave.

'Three pints and three whiskys,' I shouted to the barman as I came up to the bar and joined Colin and Jimmy.

'Steady on Billy Boy; long night ahead you know,' replied Jimmy as a way of a greeting. 'You are looking smart tonight, first time I have seen you out of a boiler suit.

'Mark of a true engineer that,' quipped Colin. 'Here's Sammy! Another round barman.'

'What about you boys? And how is our young sailor tonight?' he replied looking at me.

'Dead on Mr Agnew,' I replied taking a good slug of Guinness, as I was way behind the other two reprobates.

'Call me Sammy now Billy; next time we see you you'll be an engineer and giving us orders! Ha!'

'Don't know about that Sammy, but here's all the best and many thanks to you all for teaching me my trade,' I said toasting them.

'Aye, you were a quick learner and right up for anything we threw at you. Do you mind that auld chief that nearly had a heart attack when you told him that our apprentice had packed his stern gland Sammy?' asked Colin.

'Sure do, wanted us to re-pack it, I told him he would have to drain the dock again, and he soon shut up when I told him that he could have his next overhaul free if the gland gave any bother.'

The crack went on all night and when they threw us out at ten we went to a Chinky Restaurant and had a good curry. The boys saw me to the station and I caught the last train to Bangor, waving back as we pulled out of the station. Next thing I knew was the guard shaking me and telling me we had reached Bangor and asking if I was I wanting to stay on the train all night.

I got the telegram from trident Tankers on the following Monday. I was to join the MV *Orama* on the Wednesday in Portland Maine! Where the devil was that I thought. I looked up the atlas and found it on the East Coast of the State of Maine in USA.

My flight was tomorrow; Belfast-London, then London-Boston and finally Boston-Portland Maine. I still couldn't believe my luck as I looked at the tickets again when I was telling Ma and Da at the dinner table.

'You're very quiet Mags,' I said.

'Well child, you are so young to be going halfway across the world on your own and we won't see you again for six months. I can't believe it,' she cried and took off up the stairs.

'Never mind your sister son, we never told you before but when you were born, your Ma took a bad turn and was in hospital for a few months,' said Da, 'so she looked after you; she will miss you a lot when she makes up the pieces,' He laughed.

I went up to see big Noel and he asked me in to say cheerio to all his family. His Ma and Da were in and Jean and Hazel were just on their way out and as they gave me a big hug, I felt my first lump in my throat and my eyes started watering.

'Must have caught a cold in my eyes on the old bike,' I said to no one in particular and fled down their steps shouting farewells to Noel. 'I'll send you all cards from around the world and I will be back in about six months!' I shouted as I shut their gate behind me and headed four houses down to my own house.

I said goodnight to Ma and Da and Mags and went up to bed. My cases were all packed and I left out my flight tickets and passport for the morning. Da was running me up to Aldergrove Airport to catch the ten o'clock flight to London where I was to stay the night in the Merchant Navy Hotel and fly to America on Wednesday.

Mags came in to say goodbye, as she would be at work by the time I got up. It was very emotional, but I got through it and settled down to read a book.

Da shouted me at eight and I brought my suitcases downstairs with me.

'Going to get a good day for it, pity you didn't have time to say goodbye to the rest of the family. But you saw them all on Saturday, so I am sure they won't mind,' said Da.

Ma had the pan on and as I ate my porridge I wondered when I would get another breakfast like this one. All too soon it was time to set off and Ma gave me a great big hug.

'God be with you till we meet again my son,' she said tearfully.

'Bye Ma.' I'll phone Frankie from London and write from America before I sail if there is time. We are going to the Persian Gulf via Suez so Robert says this will take about two weeks, but I will write from there as well.'

'God bless, bye for now. Don't be crying now Ma,' I said, a lump like the Ailsa Craig forming in my throat as I loaded the cases into the boot Da's wee turquoise blue Morris Minor.

There was a bit of security to get through at the airport entrance and they wouldn't let Da into the departure lounge so we shook hands outside the terminal.

'All the best now son, take care and be sure to write to your Ma as often as you can. I am really proud of you, you have done well. Good luck! he shouted as the doors closed behind me. I looked back and waved, picked up my cases again and headed to the check-in.

I was on my way!

To follow soon

Away to Sea

by William Scott

ISBN 978-0-9570994-1-8

Turn the page for a preview…

Away to Sea

I was pressed back into my seat as we accelerated along the runway for a few minutes before we took off and we levelled out above Belfast Lough; the *no smoking and fasten seat belts s*ign went out.

I was flying from Aldergrove airport on the outskirts of Belfast to London; never having flown in my life, I was fascinated by the speed the wee plane quickly reached. I was on my way at last to join my first Merchant Navy ship as Junior Engineer and as excited as any 20 year-old boy could be on his first flight. The drinks trolley came round, but on brother Robert's advice (he had been at sea for about six years and flown all over the world – what a life!) reckoned the price of a bottle of Guinness was 3/6d, about 3 times as much as we paid in the pub at home; I therefore passed on the trolley.

I had a snack whilst looking out of the side window and noticed how green the land looked and how many shades of green there really were (is it really forty?). We went over the sea and even it was also different shades of green flecked with small white wavelets, well, until we were about half way across the Irish Sea, then it went a more blue/grey colour and the waves got bigger!

I arrived in London airport and got a taxi to The Merchant Navy Hotel, paid the taxi-man a small fortune and got a receipt. I walked up to the reception desk, thinking everyone was watching me, and announced 'Hello there, I am William Scott, booked in tonight by P & O Trident Tankers, and flying to USA tomorrow morning. I was to book an early 5a.m. call and request an early breakfast' I finished breathlessly.

(Another of brother Robert's gems of advice, order breakfast otherwise they leave out cornflakes and rolls and, cold buffet – self service) 'Sure the company picks up the tab,' I remembered him telling me.

'No bother Sir, just sign the register and put your Discharge Book I/D No. beside your name and address,' smiled the receptionist.

She must have seen thousands of seamen every year passing through the hotel on their way to meet a ship, but still managed to make me feel special.

I turned in early, slept right through despite the roar of traffic outside my bedroom window and after a good fry-up headed for the airport and it seemed in no time at all I was walking across the gangway to board a rather large jet plane; 'Boarding pass please' asked the steward, 'yes Mr Scott your seat number 47 on the inside starboard side'; fancy her knowing I was a seaman, and using nautical terms, I thought.

Soon the now familiar *safety arrangements* were over, *seat belt and no smoking signs on* and there was an almighty high-pitched whine of the turbines and then the brakes were off and this time I was nearly shoved through the back of my seat and my knuckles were white as I held onto the arms of the seat. Then bang! Up came the nose and we were in vertical take of mode; this time about twenty times faster than my previous wee propeller plane from Ireland.

I reflected on my good fortune to secure an engineers job with Trident Tankers; I would be earning about three times more a month with them than I had as a shipyard apprentice. I had set up a savings account and an allotment to my Ma at home.

I slept most of the trip and was quite refreshed when we arrived at Boston Airport and transferred to a smaller plane heading for Portland Maine.

I got talking to my neighbour on the next seat and she was from Bangor Maine; I didn't know there were several towns by that name – my own and the one in Wales. We arrived in Portland in the middle of a blizzard and soon I was standing on my own in the airport lounge waiting for the agent to come and take me to the ship. There was still no sign of him after an hour and the place looked as if it was going to close, either due to the weather or because there were no more flights that day; it was time to phone him.

I had his contact number but no change for the phone, luckily the lady in the bar lent me 10 cents!

I was relieved to get the agent first time and he was expecting my call

'Good to hear you got here all right in this weather – he sounded just like John Wayne – never knew it so bad this early in the season, anyway son, I am sending a four wheel drive to get you to the ship, you have a nice day now'. Click, the line went dead.

At last a jeep type truck drew up at the airport lounge. I don't know who was most relieved, the airport staff or myself.

The man ran into the lounge and shouted my name, picked up my case and shot back out to the jeep, I followed a wee bit slower as the snow was about knee high and drifting.

'In you get laddie, don't leave the door open or we'll freeze to death' the man shouted at me in a broad Scots accent.

'Where are you from?' I asked him

'Glasgow', he replied, 'about 20 years ago! Your ship is at the tanker berth, MV *Orama* I've got here, should be there in about half an hour if the weather doesn't worsen, how big's your ship?'

'About 60,000 tonnes,' I replied proudly.

I couldn't see a thing out of the windscreen, the wipers were really struggling to cope with the snow which now was blowing horizontally towards us, I don't know how your man saw to drive but true to his word about half an hour later we came to the tanker berth and he drove along the quay, stopping at a gangplank that disappeared upwards.

'There you go young-un, will you manage from here by yoursel?' asked my Scotsman.

'Yes, no bother at all, many thanks; I was getting a bit worried that I would miss the ship.'

I got my case from the back seat and slammed the door tight shut against the wind which was definitely getting stronger nearer the quay.

I looked up, shielding my eyes against the glare of a lamp at the top of the gangplank and nearly fell over backwards, getting a crick in my neck, she was enormous; right up out of the water so she must have finished unloading her Persian gulf crude.

I struggled up the gangplank, slipping and sliding and noticed the safety nets hanging underneath, hope I don't need those I mused; one hand for the company and one for yourself was the old yard motto.

At the top I was greeted by a deckhand, and judging by his accent yet another Scotsman, were did they all come from?

'Right Mr Scott let's have your case, you are the last aboard; I'll take you to the Chief's cabin.' He said in a not so gruff Scot's accent but still with the burrs.

'Chief, new engineer for you, just arrived from airport, looks a bit like a snowman but have to warn you he is Irish'. He shouted after knocking the Chief's door.

'Take his case to the spare juniors' cabin aft port side please Jock; I will try to instil some life back into him.'

'In you come man, you must be frozen, and we were expecting you about four hours ago, what kept you?'

'Well the agent was supposed to meet me and bring me here but he couldn't get to the airport because of the blizzard so he got a jeep to bring me,' I ventured, thinking I was getting a bollocking, but the smile on the Chief's face belied this, as he handed me a large dram.

'Get on the outside of that, William isn't it; or what do you like to be called? We call all the junior engineers 'fivers' as really anyone after fourth engineer is fifth engineer – all equal in rank,' he finished.

His accent was strange, not American but certainly not English, I didn't like to ask him though so I took a good swig of the rum and felt in burn the whole way down, making me feel a lot better.

'Right let's get you organised, follow me to your cabin, the Second usually looks after the new boys but he is down below,' he said starting off along the alleyway.

My cabin was one deck down from the Chief's and as we were leaving his cabin he pointed along the alleyway and whispered 'Old Man's cabin– want to stay away from there'.

He left me in my cabin saying that I would be on the twelve to four watch and would be called at seven bells by the junior on watch, and not to bother changing into my uniform but to make my way to the saloon for tea, just now.

I looked at my watch, I had corrected it to local time and it was already past 5 o'clock, I was getting quite peckish so I had a quick wash and kept on my suit and headed for grub.

I walked up to the bar where there were about six officers, all in uniform, standing drinking and introduced myself, wishing I had put on my uniform.

'What will you have?' asked one of the officers who had introduced everyone to me.

'Beer please' I replied

'We normally drink pink gins before dinner' replied the Second mate. (I learned later that this was a throwback from the P & O passenger liners.)

'That will do for me then,' I replied and took a good slug of the pink liquid and nearly threw it up – it tasted bitter like perfume; right lot of pansies I am in tow with here I thought.

The dinner gong sounded and we drifted into the salon. 'Over here Paddy, (news travels fast on this ship I thought) you are on my watch tonight at midnight and we will be underway by then so no more drink for us!' quipped Alex; the Third Engineer.

I had noticed a few bottles of wine dotted about the tables, but none at ours.

I was starving and dinner was great. I ate like I hadn't seen food for a week; the crack was very good. The other two lads George, the Lecky (Electrical Engineer) and Graham a deck cadet made me feel welcome and soon it was time to hit the sack and boy I needed it.

The cabin lights came on and a lad I hadn't met before was shaking me and telling me it was quarter to twelve; time for my first watch.

He introduced himself and had the audacity to ask me if I could find my way to the engine room saying he would see me down below and warning me not to go back to sleep again, as the third was a stickler for punctuality.

We must have got underway whilst I slept; I had a quick wash, jumped into a brand new white boiler-suit, picked up my piece (left in my cabin presumably by the steward) and headed for the engine room.

The ship was fairly steady but there was the all pervading heady, heavy smell of oil everywhere, even here inside the ship in the alleyway, still I was on an oil tanker.

I opened the engine room door – wow! What a racket! …

To read more, look out for

Away to Sea

by William Scott

ISBN 978-0-9570994-1-8

www.wrscottpublishing.co.uk